Effective Work

Secrets to working effectively in the
age of information overload

Dotan Nahum

Effective Work

Secrets to working effectively in the age of information overload

Dotan Nahum

Also By Dotan Nahum

Programming React Native

The Little Metrics Book

To my wife and two boys, you're my own personal A-Team.

Contents

A System for Effectiveness

Who is This Book For?

This book was written by a software professional (or at least I'd like to think!), that for the last 20 years has been doing open source consistently in pockets of free time, as well as startups.

The target audience would be anyone who appreciates time, and working effectively, and more so people who deal with software (but this is not a precondition at all).

How to Read This Book?

This bit is actually important: how to read this book depends on your persona.

- *If you're not sure*, browse through the table of contents and hunt topics that sound interesting. Do this iteratively.
- *If you have some time on your hands*, read it start to finish.

I also imagine some readers will "get" parts of this book at different phases of their life and career, so I'd encourage to get back to it from time to time.

The Age of Information Overload

Around 2007, Facebook broke out and iPhone broke out. These two disruptive products set a course for two things to happen:

1. The social Network Effect, arguably, driven primarily by Facebook. It changed how we interact with one another forever: a few years after and we have Github for our code, Slack for our discussions, Twitter for our rants, WhatsApp for our messages. The network effect also made everyone reachable to everyone and *discoverable* by everyone should they only want to be. Technologically, it pushed the world to compensate: distributed systems, big data, document stores, real-time and more.
2. iPhone made the network effect *accessible*. It changed how we interact with the digital world. It pushed the world to compensate as well: better WiFi, better cellular infrastructure, better *experiences* and better and explosive growth in software and *developer experience* driven by the new concept of Appstore.

At the start of the 2000's we were just figuring out high speed Internet so that we get to share information more effectively. Today, around 20 years later, and only about 10 years later from Facebook and iPhone, as information workers, we're at the age of information *overload*.

We're at a severe case of the *paradox of choice*: the more choices a person has, the longer it takes to decide. Big decisions are cut into low-resolution high-impact decisions. Making a decision became instant, like snapping a picture.

If that wasn't enough, then in the new age we live in, *choice creation* became more approachable as well. For example, if I'm building an ecommerce platform and I'm not sure which wording and styling will make you buy a particular product, I create 20 different product pages for it in different bundles that all generate the same profit for me and ask you to choose. I'm rephrasing the *burden* of choice as an experiment and I'm moving the hard job of decision making onto you, the *subject* of this experiment.

Just to compare, if I were a car dealer, to make you buy your next sports car from a lot of 20 different makers and colors would have been hard for me, and hard for you. I had to understand what cars I have in stock, call other dealers to make up for what I'm missing and basically ask for a favor and give them a slice of the deal, make sure to drive in the cars that I miss, service them and clean them, and finally present them to you and spend the time with you walking through their features and highlights. Lots of work for me.

Other than what we face as *users*, we have what we face as workers: *asking* you to make a choice became more approachable for the person doing the asking. All it takes is five friends and a couple of co-workers to send a message: "Lunch?" and you're spending 30 minutes trying to decide. "Did you read my email? WDYT?" pulls you from whatever you were doing, and "Send me your final design notes by tomorrow morning" through WhatsApp, iMessage and Facebook interchangeably to obliterate the time and productivity you had left for the day.

Of course these also hide some kind of bad culture such as "why the last moment notice for design notes?". You can't wonder but think about maybe the real-timeness of our new ways to communicate encourage bad cultural habits of last-minute real-time planning.

Any given tech worker today has arguably more micro decisions to make than they had five years ago, not to mention ten or twenty years ago. We have decisions that are smaller grained yet have a large effect on our work, and it's easier for others to create a decision point for us, and less and less obvious how to take a decision given the amount, shallowness and randomness of those micro decisions that arrive at our doorstep. Should we use `react-carousel` or `react-slick` or any other of the dozen available carousel components that we can use?

The whole decision cycle went upside down as well. What variant of Javascript to use for your new product that you're building? the gap between wanting to make a decision on this to making a decision is virtually just answering: "Typescript". Done. Many teams, given this decision, will run along to install Typescript, get it configured and wired throughout the project but skip the rationale. We're still learning to decide but we're not there yet, as a community.

Whether we like it or not, our industry (software) has not learned how to properly make decisions in teams. Some of the more progressive teams did learn how to do this properly, but it takes time and, ironically, it seems like a waste in the eyes of "higher ups" (ironic because bad decisions *create* waste). In some companies, a complex socio-technological paradox emerges: if you take a decision quickly without a structured logical process, you're risking the business by making a wrong and critical decision, but in the eyes of a "hip" startup CEO you come out as agile and fun and "get things done".

Truth is, we have to have both: safe *and* quick decisions. We do have that in other industries don't we?

To make good decisions you need a structured, logical process and you need attention and focus. With the Slacks and WhatsApps of the world embedded into our work day, we're losing the battle for focus and for deep uninterrupted work. It seems like society have decided that it's up to the individuals who are "productivity fans" to win this for now, and the rest can have low productivity and be micromanaged in the best case, while the worst case is to agree on a low-value-producing body as a steady-state.

It's common knowledge that a culture that supports the wrong case of micro-management often display arguing, shouting, firing people as a faux productivity tool and a toxic feedback loop of an ego boost to those who practice this.

Productivity culture is a deep, well thought out architecture of how everyone interacts and works. It is a cultural thing; and changing or building culture is hard.

You

I met investors, executives, indy hackers, and engineers and productivity fans assuming that these are the most stressed, most information overloaded and most context-switching people I can find and posed a single question: "do you meditate?".

This question started a conversation of a few hours that could go on for many more. I realized we're all in the same boat. We're all trying to solve for information overload, for poor productivity, for high demand high action environment. We all have too little time. And what we all do then, if we're lucky enough to notice, is try to understand ourselves better so that we can be more productive and effective. Mindfulness is one way, with meditation as a tool.

But this text is not about meditation. It hit me that even with these mental tools and frameworks that are available today, there's one topic you can't avoid while trying to be effective, or more generally, trying to be successful. That topic is: You. It's not possible to perfect your workflow, and you won't have a perfect time doing this, or even a good way to be effective if you don't deeply understand your values or your "baggage" whatever it may be. I realized that you have to know where you're coming from.

Find Someone Who Believes In You

You might be one of the lucky ones, that had guiding and supportive parents that believed in you. Me? it just happens that I didn't have that and it's nobody's fault. My parents were hard working, low income, rough neighborhood – I say it's a miracle I didn't end up on the streets. My mom did do one thing: she used all her savings to get me a computer and that's what changed everything for me I guess; that's how she believed in me, but then not much more than that – I didn't have all the ordinary parenting stuff that a kid should have. It was just me and the computer and I built my entire world in that computer, and I'm talking 90's here (there was no Internet yet).

I guess kids are resilient that way. Well, at least until I arrived at an age where nothing added up and my childhood story started to get in my way, I realized everyone else had a different and more happy life; that only as an adult I understood that as a family we didn't have all the means normal families had. I found that out when I was around my 30's. It's never easy to figure out something about yourself this deep and this late into the game.

This "baggage" somehow helped me create values for myself: helping others, doing without accepting any return, doing the right thing, and more – these came from the hardship of life as a kid without means. Turns out people appreciate that in a person, and as I went into my professional life, a surprising factor to me was that people believed in me and I had no idea why.

Try to find people in your life that believe in you. They might be already there but you might not even notice.

You Are a Mirror of Your Childhood

One of these people that believed in me, and I had no idea why, and I'm not sure he even knows this to the full extent that he left such an impression on me, is Gaby Bilczyk – founder of Conduit, the most successful tech company in Israel at the time, and the biggest ad-tech company in the world at the time (that would be around 2010).

On my first week or so at Conduit he came to my room – and I'm not sure he even planned this but maybe it was just a random stroll around the office – he shook my hand firmly, smiled with a whole heart and said "there are stories about you, I hope they're true. You know you have very large shoes to fill. Will you make it?". All I could think about was that I'm dressed too sloppy to shake Gaby's hand, after all I'm just meeting one of Conduit's founders!. I said "I think so... yea", without a lot of confidence. He said "You think so (friendly laugh)? nah!, you'll nail it!" I smiled back, and he smiled again. I was ready for the challenge; *someone* expected great things from me. Four years later, I became Conduit's (or; more precisely Como, the rebranded Conduit) CTO.

Years after we both parted ways with Conduit, we met casually and he heard parts of my story – my earlier story, my childhood and my struggles and before I knew it, in ways I don't fully understand how, he gave me a full breakdown of what's happening behind the covers – and it was strikingly accurate. He told me two things:

1. He told me that I'm a "street cat". I looked confused. Apparently, it means that I grew up in survival mode, I made do with what there is, and created value out of nothing because I had nothing.
2. And, that I'm a mirror of my childhood. And all people are mirrors of their childhood and there's no way to escape from that or ignore that; and that I, like all people, need to face it – whatever that means.

After this conversation, I had around two years (!) of self reflection and resolution and finally, peace. It's like I put my own self in diagnosis mode, and just resolved things with myself and got to "a-ha" moments about things in hyper speed. When you understand who you really are and where you come from, *everything* makes sense. In the end of it, I was at peace with myself. This all happened while I was deep in my professional career – which shows you it's never too late.

In the end, this helped me execute much better; focus better, and appreciate my early life better as a testament of strength instead of treating my early life and childhood as a "glitch", which I did for so many years. It also helped me understand other people better – by realizing they are a mirror of *their* childhood. By asking how *they* grew up (of course, when it was acceptable to ask), I could understand what I can do to help and be generally more accepting and understanding of things that maybe people normally see as strange.

A good way to look within is to find someone who believes in you – there's a good chance you'll find out what you're missing because they might be seeing clearly what you see partly by mistake or by choice or both.

Find What You Believe In

To prepare for effective goal settings, say, a 5-year goal, you need to know with a good degree of confidence in what you believe in, in the business sense that is.

You might believe in making loads of money, or making your first million by the age of 25. Or, you might believe in fairness, equality, or just helping people. Maybe you want to do all of those at once.

There's a good chance that you simply don't know any of that yet. Or maybe you think you know, but if you dug down into your core, it's not really what you want. I've seen that many times, a great engineer becomes a carpenter. A doctor becomes a singer. Some of us are affected by what society wants us to become; or what our parents thought of us. Whatever the reason, you owe to yourself to either (1) find your missing direction, or (2) just verify your existing direction.

We want to do all this to make sure we're propagating our directions, aspirations, from our 5-year ambition, into the day-to-day work, goals and tasks, to make it effective. All this, in order to create motivation and forceful perseverance that is unshakeable.

Your Beliefs, Timing, and Luck

Quite a few times, when I was less familiar with working effectively, I was pumped up by an idea, which turned into a project, which I validated like I should – lean canvas and "getting out of the building" and all – but months into the project it felt like I ran out of fuel; I was finding less and less reasons to keep pushing. That's because I wasn't motivated enough, it didn't connect with my values.

It's funny because many of my "dead" ideas, that I thought I executed well on and made a product out of and stopped – became a big success years later when another entrepreneur had the same idea, and got it to production, built a company out of it. One of these was something like Airtable. Because I was deep into productivity around 2009, I wanted a tool to combine several of the tools I was using – spreadsheets, note taking, ticket management. I built something like that on Rails (a web framework that exploded in popularity in and around those years, 2006-9), and dogfed on it for two years. Gave a free account to friends and it worked well as a product.

But it didn't work out – I stopped having a passion for it! Airtable on the other hand did work out, and it looks fantastic. In general, some people look at these instances of a great idea, great execution that should have worked but failed and call it a "timing problem" or maybe a "luck problem" because it's widely believed that not only do you need to have a great idea, great execution, great product market fit, and great culture – you need to have two things you can't really control – timing and luck.

Well, since I was on the inside of a few of these experiences, I can say there's also "motivation" (other people call it focus but I think a step before that is motivation). True motivation comes from what you are and what you believe in (sorry for the zen moment!); well, maybe not the ultimate zen version of that, but *some* version of that.

Some people think about it differently, they say: operate in a domain that you are a domain expert of; or in other words don't ever build a solution for a domain you know nothing about. For example, if you're a doctor don't go and build a startup for real estate – build one for healthcare.

Why is that? well, it builds upon a validated assumption – what you want to do, as an entrepreneur, is based on what you've already chosen to do as a professional or what you've already gained experience in. That you already chose something or have become knowledgeable in it means you already went through the process of selecting it, which means it's important to you, which means it somehow was part of your values.

Any way we look at it, it goes back into picking apart what you believe in and your values. But since everything is fluff talk so far – and I'm aware of that, let me humbly offer to put myself on the stand and together we can understand how all this feels and looks like on a living sample – me.

I'm not a psychologist, and there's probably an academic method-ology to do this in a better way but these are the questions I found for myself (you can use the same process for your own inspiration).

We want to touch two topics. Focusing on this:

- How did you influence others?
- How were you influenced by others?

In a slightly more low-level breakdown:

1. Others
    1. Impression you made on people. What kind of people were they? are there categories hiding? (for example: senior engineers vs junior engineers) and what kind of impression? teaching, pairing, taking work from them so that they can make the cut? and so on. Write it down on paper.

2. Impression people made on you. Try and remember which people made a good impression on you and why. Write it down on a piece of paper – that's important. Make a few iterations and take your time; and ultimately you'll be looking at a list of people that you probably want to work with in the future, and a list of things that *they* appreciate that you appreciate – and probably correlate well with your world of values; distill and document these to fine detail.

2. You
    1. What of the things you made by yourself made you the most proud?
    2. What books, videos, or any kind of knowledge that you gained influenced you the most? Can you list the material out on paper?.
    3. Do you already have a core set of values? things you've already learned that make you tick. Write these down.

You should spend around an hour with these questions. After you're done, you'll have a cluttered list of topics, ideas, people, principles all in the raw form and unprocessed.

Now to process these, you need to go over each and pick it apart to a one or two-word value.

Let's try some of it, and I'll show you how I've done it myself. I'll try to pose just one question and one answer as an example.

1. Impression I've made on people.

Removing existing infrastructure that was old-fashioned, crippling and served its creator much more than it served the people that were using it. I replaced it with great developer experience, power to the people solution. After this, engineers:

1. No longer needed someone to give them fish, they knew how to fish themselves (*don't give people fish, teach them how to fish*)

2. Were no longer blocked, they could own things end to end
3. Caught this 'bug' of being empowered, they came up with their own ideas and built their own tools
4. Could scale – teams could hire freely, unchained, not depending on one person's aging and crippling technology and knowledge

I freed up an engineering organization to be able to realize its true potential, corrected an organizational glitch, and contributed to a fair, empowering culture that helped create a great company (I know because I was there to see it transform, which was amazing). Furthermore, I discovered that by empowering people without asking for returns – gains you friends for life that remain friends even when either of you change workplaces. Great friendship trumps workplaces (companies come and go).

Let's break down the raw data that I've drafted above. Treating it as raw text and extracting value, I come at a first iteration:

- Doing the right thing
- Putting a stop to people who have misplaced or unproductive intentions
- Teaching people to solve their own problems
- Empowering people
- Make people do more with the help of technology
- Make friends
- Being a good person
- Building an efficient organization
- Enabling success
- Seeing what everyone else are too busy to see, seeing the 'patterns' and 'design smells'

Second iteration, let's group related items:

Doing the right thing, or good karma.

- Doing the right thing
- Putting a stop to people who have misplaced or unproductive intentions
- Being a good person
- Make friends

Empowering other people.

- Teaching people to solve their own problems
- Empowering people
- Make people do more with the help of technology

System thinking, engineering, mechanics of logic.

- Seeing what everyone else are too busy to see, seeing the 'patterns' and 'design smells'

Striving for success.

- Building an efficient organization
- Enabling success

And now the final extra step, let's pick just one or two words to describe each category:

1. Good Karma
2. Empowering others

2. System thinking
3. Success

Apparently, from the analysis above and based not on all of the questions, but just on one or two questions I've asked myself here – this is what I'm about: Karma, empowering others, systematic thinking, and success.

Can I validate this? well, sure. The Karma part or "do good" part comes from the fact that as a kid I had what I thought of an unfair life and well, my childhood was a journey of correcting unfairness. Empowering others – came directly from this vivid example of unlocking a whole engineering group, after which my course of professional life changed. I discovered what it feels like to unchain people; to free people to fulfill their own professional potential. Systems thinking – I have no idea where that came from, but since early childhood I have always been a logical person. Maybe because my father, who was a car mechanic, had me repairing cars with him since early age? I don't know; but that's a start to figure this one out that I guess I'll have to carry with me some more time to get a clear idea.

Finally, the 'success' part definitely comes from my mom; who made me do my homework no matter what; when we were in a single bedroom apartment, or in times of war (that would be Gulf War), or in times of financial stress. Homework trumped all; no excuses; no nothing. The principle here, I guess, wasn't the homework, but to be successful in *something* despite everything else; or maybe the less galant answer is that making me do my homework every day was just a distraction for her – a way to take her mind off the day-to-day stress and focus on something less stressful such as algebra. But for me, I understood that I need to achieve success despite of all the hardships. When other kids had fun, had the means to have fun, or more generally had the supportive infrastructure to be kids – I was doing hard work; homework, repairing cars, or helping around the house.

And to tie this all down, keeping in the mantra of "you are a mirror of your childhood", well I had a hard childhood, and in my honest opinion too early and too hard. As a kid, I remember having a feeling of "life is unfair" when all other kids were just having fun being kids. This triggered a question of "how can I make life fair?" that surrounded me with everything I did as a kid; I wanted to create a fair world. Maybe some days I wish I had that wall-street guy mindset with this built-in hunger to make money because that's all I saw my parents do as a child, but I have to accept that that's me, and maybe – if I choose to – plot a course towards a different reality that *starts* from these stepping stones of personality and doesn't ignore them.

This is me!

1. Good Karma
2. Empowering others

   2. System thinking
   3. Success

What values hide in you? go ahead and try this exercise!

Are You Effective?

There are signals that relate to yourself, and those that related to people surrounding you. How effective you are works as a system in the systems-theory sense, you influence your environment and your environment influences you; and so we want to isolate each part and look at each in turn. See if you can identify yourself in either of these below.

Procrastination

Humans, and perhaps all living things, want to consume a good amount of energy and spend as little amount of it as possible; because part survival is about keeping this equation honest: not spending more energy than you should. Procrastination is a way for our brain to convince us to do that; we prefer checking our inbox and deleting promotional emails instead of checking our inbox and replying to important emails regarding important matters. We prefer browsing through Amazon, shopping for "important" equipment – for anything really – rather than doing the honest research on what our requirements really are, if we even require anything, that is; or some times we prefer spending time on doing research because it takes our minds off replying to important emails – you can mix and match. It's a clever system our brain uses and often it wins us over. Often you can't really know you're procrastinating because it comes with such a sophisticated reasoning system; your brain will be more than happy to supply reasons why what you're doing is not really procrastination.

My wallet was falling apart, after serving me for about 15 years. My intuition was that I have to get something that'll be *that* good

– that's sentiment springing into action, not reason.

Yet, I decided I'm going to *understand* wallets. Apparently, there's a whole world out there for wallet connoisseurs – bifold, passport, slim wallets, full grain leather, handmade leather, lifetime warranty, and boutique shops and even some kind of hyper-boutique shops which make wallets with the same methods they did a hundred years ago for whatever that means.

I spent almost a full weekend on that. Even though I'm well versed on procrastination and effectiveness; my brain won me over – "this makes sense!" it said. Eventually, *because* I'm aware of what procrastination is, I woke up to the voice of reason. I made a decision and bought *two* wallets and stopped debating which of the two is better and so cut off the paradox of option. I ended up giving one of them as a present to a friend.

I could have been done in an hour, but it took a weekend. At least it didn't take a full week. Being a guitar collector, some guitars took me a month or more to make up my mind on. So, could have been worse. So how did I force myself to stop?

1. Being aware of the problem of procrastination is 50% of the battle. If you're aware of it, and you're mindful of too much time spent on *any thing*, then you have your first signal: "something's wrong!". If you're doing a single thing for more than a day, that signal should be there.

2. Ask yourself – since time is money, how much have I spent already? if you're researching what kind of bike helmet to buy, and they're typically $40-$100, but you're not sure if to get the more expensive one and you're doing this for the last couple days on your free evenings for a total of 5 hours, and your hourly rate is $80, you've just spent $400 on trying to optimize a purchase. Break off early, buy the $100 one, and avoid the extra spend in hours. Even if evenings are not a billed hourly time, and your rate isn't $80, it's still worth to be calculating your decisions this way.

Your Environment

If your environment (people, working area, tools) is not effective, and you interface with it in order to do your job – you won't be effective as well.

Taking care of your environment has never been more important, since the network effect made our environment hyper-connected, available, and very, very noisy both in terms of actual noise and noise as irrelevant information. Odds are that, say in an engineering organization, you won't be able to change your environment that much if you're one engineer out of a few hundred because that's simply going against the grain, but you *can* set a standard towards how to interface with *you* and what you expect from others.

For example, I largely treat WhatsApp (or any kind of instant messaging) as a pull-based thing. I don't accept the fact that I should immediately answer messages because that's how it works, and so I check messages on a schedule that I'm comfortable with and that is still reasonable towards others.

Most people would be OK if you answer within a day or within 12 hours, so checking messages once a day would be reasonable.

This requires some preparation and expectation setting, because you're breaking a cultural and social habits. You should tell people you have a different way to do messaging, and how to still get a hold of you when matters are urgent – I recommend the old and faithful *phone call*. It makes the person calling you invest substantial effort (remember the thing about humans being naturally conserving of energy?), and this person will (1) double-check if they want to actually make the call, and if it's important enough and (2) when they do make the call, you'll have their full focus, and they'll have yours and (3) often messages are a poor way to move information from side to side. According to studies, as much as 50% of text messages are misunderstood because of the lack of tone amongst other things) so you'll get better communication on what we've proved to be – urgent matters.

Effectiveness Systems

Graphic designers have discovered *design systems* in the last few years. This is the idea that design (I'm also a part designer) is something that needs structure, a system to automate it, make it efficient and effective, communicate, hand off and standardize design. We've been doing things like design hand-off in the wrong way in the software industry for a bunch of years so far (did I tell you the story about that one time when a designer saved a '.gif' as a '.png' by mistake and engineers ended up rebuilding our rendering engine?).

I'd say the "modern" requirements for hand-off came when the mobile market became a thing, somewhere around 2007. We just didn't have enough time as an industry to figure out and understand that sending out a PSD file to a developer isn't helping that developer at all because suddenly, there are around ten different screen sizes and image formats to support and this person has no idea about these. And that shipping low-res pixels to production for hi-res screens aren't a good example of a healthy software lifecycle; if it made it to production, *everyone* in the software supply chain need to undo and redo their part. And in fact it seems to be a simple tooling problem.

What about... work systems? or maybe, since we're also dealing with our own individual self and not a team – so we don't confuse with waterfall, scrum and agile – let's call it effectiveness systems? What about effectiveness systems? did anyone ever tell you how you should organize your working day? Or how you can make the most out of a working hour?

Precisely.

A Word About Going Indy

Going indy, that is, deciding that you are a one man show that will ideate, plan, prioritize, produce, execute, verify, ship, and learn from your own mistakes in order to, well, build your own business and make it profitable, is an *extreme* private case of just being a productive and an effective individual.

There's something interesting about going indy and looking at how effective work takes a high priority. If you decide to go indy, this is one equation you have to answer for:

```
1   (time + money) / ( bizdev +  scope x (product + UI + PM +\
2    dev + QA + BI + marketing + infra) )
```

Notes:

- `product` - product management, prioritization, grooming backlog, planning, thinking about new ideas.
- `PM` - project management, understanding what should come first, what are the risks, blockers, resources needed, and *how* to execute.

First, let's understand what components take the most time. Here's the top 3:

1. `dev` - development time, or: time building things.
2. `infra` - infrastructure time, or: making sure you and your product can run properly in a predictable manner.
3. `bizdev` - business development, or: finding new clients.

Next, what components take the most amount of money, here's the top 3:

1. `dev` - time is money and you'll be spending a lot of it here.
2. `marketing` - running ad campaigns, paying for publicity and so on.
3. `bizdev` - flights, conferences, custom demos RND time.

Now assuming you have a fixed amount of time and money, and you have not a lot of wiggle room in life; what can you do with what you've already got?

Here are some ideas that people usually adopt:

- You can be the engineer and not do bizdev at all (that is: don't spend time on meeting people to build a network), and that's arguably risking having a momentum once you have something ready.
- You can run fast and break a lot of things by simply not doing quality (e.g. less infra).
- You can ask a friend to do some of the work (delegate).
- You can reduce scope. Many times this would be the 'right' thing to do, but you risk missing the market.
- You can work *smarter*, but that's kind of a voodoo to nail, right?

This book deals with how you can work in a smarter way, how you can rethink *scope*, or more generally it will let you:

1. Understand scope and goals
2. Understand yourself
3. Understand effective work and execution

Time

Set Your Time Expectations

There's a consensus about humans not being able to estimate well, also known as the *optimism bias* or simply our tendency to disregard historical events and so we're not estimating based on past experience but on what's happening right now and what we would wish from the future to happen *[Biases and Corrective Procedures Tversky and Kahneman, 1977]*. Where it meets us is that we now know that people are overly optimistic about how much they can do in a given block of time. From this logic comes that we're all probably stuck trying to do a lot in a day, ending up doing a small fraction of our tasks at hand and then we feel frustrated about our effectiveness.

It's not just about our biases – there are the "peripheral" issues that hurt your ability to reason about time and execute effectively such as: unpredictable tasks throughout the day, family, kids, fatigue, being sick, phone calls, instant messaging and so on. All these are around you, challenging your productivity 24/7, and are actively impairing your probably-good-on-paper ability to estimate correctly *even if* you're immune to human biases (you're probably not).

There are plenty of techniques to improve your ability to estimate and execute. Using other people to check your estimates, averaging a few estimates to form one, marking up unknowns and integrating risk as a buffer estimate, and more. Also what helps is acknowledging that even when you estimate correctly, you might not predict your ability to execute on it. For example, with Agile and Scrum, we're subtracting days that people are expected to take a vacation and we're creating this fluid concept of *capacity*, which means at any given time we know how much execution power we have, and expectations around our capacity are set and so we have increased our chances to meet our expectations.

But ultimately we want to talk about our own effectiveness and productivity, we talk about the individual, often without an ability to average a full-house estimates of a team, or have someone to double-check our treatment of time. How do we make enough time? how do we hit the goals that we set for the day in an effective way? Or more on the feelings side, how can we not feel disappointed at the end of the day?. The short answer is: it's complicated. The slightly longer answer is: let's do an exercise.

But first – you can't have *more* time. Sorry. There's a glass-ceiling for your execution power (which we will help you get closer to with this book, but you'll have to smash it by yourself); because even if you were the smartest and most efficient person in the world, you'd arrive at a point where it's physically not possible to do things quicker in order to push more things into a day and then meet all of your goals.

Understanding the above, let's start our exercise: say you want to work on something fun for yourself. Take 24 hours and start reducing the hours that you can't optimize for. 8 hours of sleep puts you at 16. 8 hours of day job puts you at a remaining 8. 30 minutes of shower, 30 minutes of dinner, an hour of family time puts you at a remaining 6 hours. Let's say commute takes an hour for each direction so you're at 4 hours that you have left. Let's put an hour as a buffer: all kinds of errands around the house (shopping, dishes, cleanups). You're at 3 hours. Working in a startup for 10 hours instead of 8? you're at a pitiful *one hour* left. Not working in a startup but had a glitch at work and stayed for 9 hours instead of 8? you're looking at 2 hours. But let's not get too gloomy – let's keep a nice work-life balance of 8 hours at work; and, as we've computed – 3 hours of free time daily to use to work towards your own goals and ambitions.

That's 3 hours of work if you're committing to the *bare minimum* of what we describe as our day-to-day. No TV, not more than an hour of family time, no social networks of any kind and no socializing. No casual phone calls with friends. No maintaining your professional network by attending meetups and professional events.

If you sleep less, say 7 hours, and maybe find a way to have a different kind of dinner, say on the road, you'll manage to gain 1.5 hours.

You see where this is going. There's not much to play with and there are the rigid, non-flexible commitments: work and sleep and the "flexible" commitments such as dinner (in the sense that although it's a bad thing to do, you can skip dinner some time but cannot skip a full-night sleep).

Write down on paper all the time boxes that's "flexible". Try to understand how are the other 8 hours of daily time being spent? how's your commute? is it *really* one hour? every time? how long do you shower? and anything you can think of really. See what kind of numbers you're left with, and if you're having the same number each day consistently, or, you basically depend on some random factor of how your day goes which influences how much time you have left. For example, if your commute is prone to traffic jams, then your free time will be unpredictable.

After you're done recording everything on paper, you should have a good clue if you:

- Have some free time at all
- Have free time that is *stable* in the sense that you can trust that 3 hours is 3 hours every day
- Have a general sense for if the world around you can deliver you stable and consistent chunks of time (good) or not (bad)

Now comes realization. Chances are that you have little time left each day and that you must've negotiated with yourself to failure (you can't win more time, you'll realize this after a few minutes), and understood there's nothing you can do about it other than agree that these poor 3-odd hours you have left is all there is. There's a single conclusion: you have to be effective with what you have. Not only you have very little time and a lot to do, you just found out this time is actually incredibly precious and perhaps not even stable and consistent (one day you have it, one day you have traffic jams and it goes away).

By the way we just credited 2 hours for commute. If you work remotely or move to some place closer, you can win these back. Also, if you can work while commuting (e.g. train), you can win these back.

The basics are in place. There's things you can't change (sleep), things you can negotiate yourself out of (work, commute), and things you better not negotiate out of but there's people who do (family time, shower), and then there's the time you have left. Do your math and try to negotiate more out of this time, using the ideas here.

The rest of this book is about the time you do have left each day and how to use it the most effectively.

Avoid Time Sinks

Avoiding time sinks and failing fast are related. In systems design, a fail-fast system is one which stops and reports errors immediately as opposed to continue to operate in some hope it'll recover or that some kind of process will recover it. Startups and hi-tech companies have also embraced "failing fast" in a way that's inspired by fail fast systems.

In principle there are tradeoffs at play here:

- Fail fast because you don't have time to invest in the "chance" of success. You prefer restarting, having a clean slate, and believe that often a clean slate and more energy into new starts can carry the momentum for better probability for success.

- Fail slow because you have time to invest in the "chance" of success. You prefer staying course, because for some reason you believe that it would be overly expensive to restart and that you've invested too many resources in the current direction.

This also has ties with the Innovator's Dilemma *[Innovator's Dilemma, Clayton Christensen, 1997]*, which deals with how great companies can do everything "right" and yet still lose their market leadership. These companies would prefer staying course, one reason being that they cannot assemble the resources (for political or financial reasons) needed for doing a restart. But there's more to it, sometimes it is *smarter to stay course*; maybe you're building a startup to optimize diamond cutting – would you throw away diamonds?

The answer to this dilemma is:

1. Understand your market dynamics, your gains and your waste. If you're a carpenter, or you're in diamond cutting – every wrong cut is a critical waste. If you're in software, and it's built right, you can have virtually no waste which leads to the next principle
2. If you want to fail fast, you must build for failure. Have the proper infrastructure to fail fast; in software, that would be test coverage, proper architecture and treating software as craft.

In the context of working effectively, our dynamics are the same as any other startup. We're overloaded with goals and tasks and have too little time and resources. Which is why we need to do everything we can to fail fast and build our time management workflow around failing fast: design experiments, build spikes, draft designs and quick sketches and to find ways to evaluate these quickly. Don't build a product until you have to and build the tools and practices to allow quick experiments, and move from an idea to a sketch to code to product in a minimal amount of steps.

One of the products that disrupted how I fail fast was an iPad Pro with Apple Pencil. I found that investing in these tools pays itself multiple times over because it creates a natural interface between my ideas and sketches and most importantly handing these to the digital world. It helps in capturing ideas, building visual presentations, demos, animations and more without the overhead of transferring from paper, or being limited to building slide decks in order to convey ideas. If I can get an idea and a sketch out faster, I can accelerate failing because I just saved time on the way for building a POC.

I also use starter projects for everything. These are my own custom-built boilerplates built to accelerate going from idea to product. I take *significant* time to build and maintain my own starter projects for every scenario. Be it a command line app, an iOS app or a full-stack SaaS app; anything I can sell. When I have an idea to test, I generate a starter project and I'm starting "hot" into my idea instead of dealing with a "getting started" syndrome for a long while.

When the time comes to reach a market, I use static website generators which allow me to generate any kind of MVP, drop it in an S3 bucket and my own domain and have a launch-rocket like experience with paying almost nothing. The bonus is that if it takes off, unlike custom "launch your startup" platforms and website builders, I have *again* a boosted start: the material I've created will be used as the foundations of the new product, I can continue pushing hot into the idea rather than start from scratch.

In addition, when you plan to build something new, identify and tackle the harder or unknowns first. Perform a structured risk assessment and mitigation process head-on. One way I do this is by outlining my assumptions and proving them. All you need are a few bullets:

- **Background**. One paragraph describing your pain points and a bit of context and history.
- **Motivation**. One paragraph *justifying* our goal of solving the pain points that were described earlier.
- **Assumptions**. A list of all of your assumptions. This is tricky to identify but a rule of thumb is that you should try to challenge every "fact" that you state. This challenge mixed with your "fact" is your assumption. For example *"A flashlight application will be used by everyone and so we have a very wide addressable market"* to be challenged by "Well, people might not have LEDs that can be programmable", and be stated as "Assuming users have the correct hardware, a flashlight application is something they will use". Keep iterating on it as many times as you need until you feel all of your assumptions has been recorded.

The goal of recording your assumptions is twofold:

1. You want to be able to pivot quickly. You can only pivot *from* something *to* something if you know precisely what you're pivoting *from*. The worst thing that can happen is that you pivot and pivot again and find yourself building that same product that failed just under a different story or pitch. If you know exactly what your assumptions are and which ones were invalid, you know where to go.
2. You'll be able to fail fast. Sometimes you don't know *when* you failed and what's your definition of failing. Your natural momentum will want to carry forward even though there's glaring signs of failure, and this also relates to the biases we've covered in this book. If you have a list of assumptions, you'll know exactly which ones are failing at any given moment if you stare at these from time to time.

- **Goals**. One primary goal and a few secondary goals. You must have just one primary goal. For example, a primary goal of *"Build the company's new marketing website"*, with a secondary goal of *"If we use a new modern tech stack, it can jumpstart new product features"* and so the goal is "Use new tech stack".

Switch Context Effectively

We all switch context to varying degree, and context switching is widely accepted as a productivity killer, as discussed in *["Maker's Schedule, Manager's Schedule"*[1], *Paul Graham, 2009]*. Here's an idea, if we *must* switch context, how can we do it effectively?One way I keep track is that I maintain a *worklog*, where I record the highlight of what I worked on during the day. Note that people that bill hourly have this as part of how they do billing, by-design.

A recording of what you're doing will serve as breadcrumbs for you to remember where you were when you left something. I use Evernote for my worklog, and it will look like this:

- #golang upgraded Go to 1.13
- #hygen cover all open issues, merge PRs

Other than a worklog, I also *leave the door open*. It means that before I leave a project for a while, I make sure there's an easy-entry task left to take when I pick it up again. Whether I'm not working on it for a day, a week or a month I'll use a different way to remind my future self where to start. For example, I leave a breaking build if I know I'm taking a short break from a project which is a few days up to a week.

For longer breaks, I keep the project in pristine condition, clean it up, and write proper documentation to state where I left, what

---

[1]http://www.paulgraham.com/makersschedule.html

needs to be done, and any contextual information that's important that I know I'm going to need in the future, as well as the last few actions in a worklog format. For this I tend to use a non-formal, loose language like I'm talking to myself; I found from experience that this is the fastest way to catch up – you may want to experiment and decide for yourself what kind of writing style you want to use.

Learn to Shut Down

Today's "social norms" create a reality in which people expect you to be always available to instant messages. Many times these interactions which start with a question-reply take longer than that because instant messaging is a very easy format to communicate in; the mental cost of sending a message is virtually nothing. In the general sense, the cost of instant messaging is severely under-estimated as shown in *["The effect of instant messaging services on society's mental health", Rosenbaum and Wong, 2012]*. In the context of effective work, instant messaging takes you out of focus and creates an information management overhead as you keep track of all of your chats in your head, and ultimately, gives you more to do.

To deal with this you need to take a stance against these unfortunate "social norms" and pick your *shut down strategy*. At first I started shutting down on my own initiative without notifying anyone. I didn't answer immediately but I answered when I felt I can invest the time and focus, and educated people that this is my instant messaging dynamic. I also removed all tracking facilities: the read-confirming blue tick boxes from WhatsApp and my online status, I added an addon to block read-receipt in Gmail that blocks a wide array of email tracking pixels (if you didn't know, many people and mostly salespeople, use tracking pixels to see if you've read an email they sent you; the tracking pixel is covert, and bluntly speaking, is a way of spying on you).

You don't need others to track you, and you know what? you don't need to track others either (some apps will deny you tracking others if you shut down other's abilities to track you). I find, and I hope you will too, that it's much less stressful that way in any case. I check emails *once* daily, answer WhatsApp a couple times daily and *not* in real time, and I've shut down or stopped using any other forms of messaging and social networks: iMessage, Facebook, LinkedIn and so on.

But there's also a risk to this, like every time you're pulling yourself from an acceptable society norms. If you have people that are business partners, or partners in an initiative you're running – you can't shut down one-sidedly. What you need to do is tell them and set expectations about how you implement effective work. Educate them about the fact that you're practicing effective work, and this is part of the program. It's just another thing like Inbox Zero, like Scrum, like GTD. Tell them this is how you make a day worth 25 hours and not 24.

If you do that, you let people know more or less when you're available, and what are the "emergency" routes for communication, and they hopefully will appreciate your work ethics and that you're finding a better, more effective ways to work – maybe they'll adopt it too.

Know How To Ask and Answer

Let's say someone asks you for advice, this person says something along the lines of "I need your help designing a data lake for ecommerce that involves scraping, cleaning, normalizing public information as well as being able to slice and dice information efficiently".

There are many ways to start answering this question, ranging from:

- A cafeteria answer, that's mainly an idea, hand waving and a no-strings attached answer
- A whiteboard session that outlines an architecture of a valid idea, but that requires POCs and strong validation
- A detailed system design top-down that leaves no stone unturned
- A working product and implementation that works generically but needs some adaptation to work to requirement
- A custom build, fully operational product that is perfectly built to requirements

In many cases, the person asking *nor* the person answering knows exactly what kind of answer they want.

It might be that the person asking only wants a whiteboard session but you're deep diving so hard that you lost your audience.

It might be that you're giving a whiteboard session but you've let down the person asking because this person already got a few of those and they're looking for details.

How to tackle this? I have a system that describes the mental state of the person asking that can help you set expectations in a better way. It assumes the asking person's needs revolve around a few dimensions:

- How
- Capacity
- Focus
- Results

So for example, if I'm the person asking, I might already know *How* I want to do something, but I don't have the capacity for it. In that sense, I'm looking for working hands that's skilled for the work.

In another instance, I might know How to do something, and have a team ready to go, and have the mental focus to deep dive when needed, but I might not know how results should look like. For example, if I want to have a company be GDPR compliant, and I have my focus, engineers to work on this project already allocated, and I know how to solve for it from an engineering point of view, but I'm not sure what the end state looks like from a regulation point of view, I would pick up a counsel to help show me what the end result should be.

What I usually do, if time allows is to tell the person asking that this is my framework of thought. It helps put things in the right boxes.

After that, I try to figure out what of the four dimensions is expected and to set that expectation before diving in.

With the years, I found that this simple trick saves a lot of time and front to back discussions just to figure out where each one of the asking/answering system stands.

Flow

Finding flow is hard if you want to find flow *consistently*. You probably know when you had a great day, because it feels like you had a great day, but odds are that you don't really know what made it a great day. Which means, it's hard to reproduce.

Don't Prepare To Start, Just Start

I'm a strong believer in improving how your work space, environment, and tools affect your productivity, your mood, and your ability to execute. From having a clean and tidy workstation, to your own wide array of tools specially crafted, to having a quiet place to work that feels warm and calm. I spent time picking the right type and color of wood for my custom-built desk, the right mechanical keyboard (I went through five different mechanical keyboards until I found what worked best for me), the right chair, and the right screen.

I also believe in a clean desk as a driver for a clear mind; so I take extra care to keep my desk clean and remove objects that get randomly scattered around as I work.

But like everything: there's a balance to keep here. I discovered that sometimes I'll invest in cleaning my home office, arranging stuff, tidying up, just before sitting down to start my daily work, and that it slowly turned into a form of procrastination! What a sophisticated device is the human mind: it took something I strongly believed in, that helped me be more productive, and turned it – without my noticing – into procrastination, the enemy of productivity. Your brain will do a lot to avoid friction, to avoid challenges, messy things, complicated things, risky things, or more generally: to avoid anxiety. This is just how it works [*"The Genetics of Health", Paul, 2017*].

After noticing this "trick", I forced myself to stop "preparing" for work. If I have a task – I sit down in whatever environment there is, and only after I'm fired up and in the zone, perhaps 10-15 minutes after working on this task, I find a small pocket of time to do that clean up that I used to do as a precondition for starting work. This way I don't "fall in love" with cleaning up and preparing for work. In some occasions I work in a messy environment on purpose as an antidote for this pitfall.

In a way, not being able to start is a result of one side of an equation with two variables winning. These two variables are:

1. Fear of making a mistake
2. Fear of not acting

As long as (2) is not scary enough, you'll be in analysis paralysis. If needed, simulate (2) – set a deadline, or commit yourself publicly or to friends and family.

Adopt an Execution Framework

You might not have noticed it but you might already have an execution framework that you use for your daily ceremonies: waking up, brushing teeth, shower, morning coffee, lunch, and so on. These fixed events in your day keeps you from appearing at work in your pajamas, for example.

Getting Things Done (abbrev. GTD) is a great framework to base your *execution framework* on in order to, well, get things done. While GTD goes to great depth to describe how you should organize your life, you can make do with just the process and mindset that it introduces to make sure you have a system of execution that you can follow daily.

In that sense, GTD is a system of processing and workflow optimization, with the purpose of offloading the burden of maintenance from your brain. The idea is that if you have a system, your brain becomes a processor, not a janitor. Your brain will be free to be used for the tasks at hand. While there are other methodologies to try, I urge you to try and stick to GTD as a baseline; you can go and learn it in 15 minutes[2].

Motivate Yourself Relentlessly

Your mind needs fuel. Healthy food and spiritual and mental fuel are great, but to keep producing effectively you need *motivational* fuel: something to keep you inspired. Incidentally, this is something that would correlate with your values (you have to have values of your own. there's a whole section on this later in the book). Invest in experiences that give you motivation such as helping people with needs or try public speaking so that people get to learn something new that you can teach and get inspired by you: inspiring others is a strong way to get inspired.

Then, make it "stick". Which means find a process that works for you so that you keep practicing getting motivated.

For example you can set a process to:

- Document, file and consume motivational material:
  - Keep your own clips of motivation to watch from time to time. Steve Jobs' commencement speech[3] is one of my favorites, and in fact *most* commencement speeches are very inspiring

---

[2]https://hamberg.no/gtd/
[3]https://www.youtube.com/watch?v=UF8uR6Z6KLc

- Inspiring TED talks
- Inspiring shows and movies. I'm very picky about what I watch
- There's inherent motivation when creating stuff from scratch: the joy of creation
- Sometimes to kickstart a new hobby or habit it helps to attach a money amount to what you produce just to make it a bit more real. "It would be nice to take on photography and *actually*I saw pictures sell for $20 on stock photos, maybe I'll do that while I'm learning to shoot photos."
- Set up a process to write and publish posts regularly. Same principles work here as talking on stage: sharing with others and helping others learn is often inspiring
- Keep a portfolio of talks that are fully transcribed and if possible recorded. Talks that you re-do are the easiest and most effective and there's nothing like a talk you already gave, to give to a newer audience to understand what you need to improve. Often with these, you don't work as hard to prepare, you aren't stressed because of the crowd, and you already fixed the talk with earlier crowd feedback
- Set up a process to find meetups and to talk at these meetups

Explore and Experiment

There are two categories of tasks that deserve special attention. They deserve special attention because these are the ones that in the pressure of time and stress, get tossed away.

Let's see what *categories* of tasks we have if we try to bucket them into actions that we take in general:

1. Errands - from groceries up to clearing up your desk. Great for low energy, low mental energy

2. Prioritization - Making sure your runway is clear and you know what's next. Decide what's important and what makes better impact and what should go first
3. Planning - Incubating ideas, researching, talking to people, giving yourself some hard time courtesy of your olympic self. Also, lining up your next batch of tasks, or: planning your sprint
4. Execution - Grunt work of solving problems, writing code, building stuff. Picking off items from your sprint
5. Reflection - Stopping to reflect, understand how's your execution engine is built
6. Rest - Rest time.

And finally, guess what's easy to overlook?

7. Exploration
8. Experimentation

Or more fondly we can call this: "play time". Not in the sense of finding ways to kill time, but *play time* in that primal sense of experimentation and learning directly from failing, and learning from doing.

Exploration and experimentation are a bit different because we can't immediately see their ROI (return on investment). However, these two categories of tasks are what often brings us to break walls, shatter glass ceilings, or overcome writer's block, or more generally, have better ideas than what we already have or augment our existing ones. Exploration and experimentation allows us to challenge our neurons in a very effective way.

Exploration is learning from reading, seeing, hearing and discovering. For example, for me, exploration includes being able to consume news for my world of content.

I wanted to make sure that only news that are worth their value in reading time arrive at my inbox. For that I built a custom pipeline where top content from crowd-sourced news platforms like Reddit and Hacker News gets arranged and curated automatically into a daily email digest which is later sent by this automated process to myself. I try hitting at least two of the emails I get in each week day to get synced up, and it was worth the time building this automation as well as enjoying the fruit of this labor: I get new ideas, new research leads, and blockage lifted.

Experimentation is learning through practice and failure. You need to be able to experiment with ideas, try out new things, new technologies, new approaches, new hardware, new ways of life.

Like everything about productivity, there's a catch – if the process of exploration is "heavy", you risk never getting it done or never feeling excited about it so you'll have to make sure that for yourself you've removed the obstacles and the heaviness from experimentation. Funny enough, but when I was trying to hack myself into jogging more frequently, I read that it's a good habit to prepare your running shoes and jogging outfit beforehand next to your desk so I did that, and it worked; the hack, more generally, worked on making something more *available*.

Instead of getting up, finding my shoes, sifting through my closet and the whole shebang, I reduced it just: get dressed and go out. Since then, I look around and find ways to improve *experience* around things to make them more effective – one that stuck is improving developer experience.

For example for building software products effectively, I've built a power-pack project for every programming language I'm working with (that makes around 6-7 different packs), where the experience is that I just clone the project and I'm ready to code and start experimenting *productively* within a second. My bar for "productively" is set fairly high: in some projects I invested around two weeks in total in creating the infrastructure for *fast* iteration, precise delivery and amazing developer experience.

In practice, it means you want to add a mantra to your day to day:

build your toolbox. Your toolbox is what will put you in the top percentile of productivity. It also helps to add this category of items into your sprint explicitly.

I try setting a *goal* called E&E explicitly for this. One more trick I use, since I have already a fairly efficient workflow, is batching exploration and experimentation items together. So in one sitting, during an hour or two I can explore 4-5 different items at once, make my mental notes, and get follow-ups. And so it helps to keep *one* task or ticket that holds 4-5 of exploration and experimentation items.

Groom and Optimize Your Tools

Earlier, we discussed how cutting down the barrier to exploration and experimentation can unlock a world of effectiveness. But what about cutting down the barrier for your daily work? If you identify what you spend the most time with in terms of tools and ways of working, and invest the time to do it properly it can pay off.

The idea is to cut down barriers. Taking some thoughts from Zen and the Art of Motorcycle Maintenance[4], here's what I find important if you choose programming as your "destiny", so to speak.

- Use a strong machine that doesn't take long to compile. This one's a classic and in general: put more money into your tools to gain your time back, and in turn, you'll eventually get your money back in the form of more work done. Don't accept waiting for a build
- Learn your editor, or use Vim. The idea that you spend almost all of your time *in an editor* is one that, strangely, some people tend to overlook. Invest in learning Vim, it'll be one of the *only* things that you invest in, that you can keep for decades

[4]https://en.wikipedia.org/wiki/Zen_and_the_Art_of_Motorcycle_Maintenance

- Learn to touch type, and get a quality mechanical keyboard or a keyboard that creates zero friction between you and your computer
- Understand what addons and tools can save you time. If there's a problem in the world, chances are someone has already built a product for that right? well, most of the time that's true. You might not even have noticed everyone is using this great new productivity tool and you're actually doing things the old way. Keep exploring for ways to improve even when you think there's no more ways to improve
- Adopt a productive work paradigm. For programming, one of these would be test-driven-development; other than the essential software qualities, you'd be surprised that it's simply a *productive* way to work
- Learn proper engineering. Everyone can code, but not everyone are doing engineering. Things like SOLID, DRY and domain driven design are the flavors of "engineering standards" that you can use in order to produce better software which in turn will make for more productive time
- Invest in screen real-estate. This one too is a classic; don't waste time moving between app windows or looking for the right one. Make sure everything you're working on is in front of you and directly visible

Keyboards and Screens

As a technology worker, say programmer or engineer – there's a high chance there are two components besides a workstation that if you properly invest in, you'll get some productivity back. Sure you can invest in a beast of a computer: fast CPU, lots of RAM; but today with Macs you're almost on a safe bet if you get the high-ends (Macbooks are able to be fully spec'd out typically in their larger screen variants – say, 16"). Next, your screen. Screens used to be a big deal as well, who remembers CRTs? Today a good 27" or 30" screen is worth a fraction of what it used to be. One of these is great, a couple is even better for your productivity.

Keyboards are the tougher adaptation to make. I recommend a mechanical keyboard and to learn to touch type. On the matter of *keyboard layouts*, I used Dvorak for a while but folded back to QWERTY. The whole process was very painful and took a year and a half to unlearn QWERTY, learn Dvorak, and unlearn Dvorak and learn back QWERTY. The lesson of this experience is that I know exactly what it looks like at the other end of the keyboard layout river; I had to see if it worked for me and I was ready to invest a year of hardship to learn that lesson. Keyboard layouts are an individual thing, I guess, and you have to put a considerable amount of time to see if it's for you.

So, even if you swap a layout or not, a couple things remain: get a mechanical keyboard and learn to touch type. The mechanical keyboard debate is full of fallacies and myths. I leave all the "faster typing" arguments aside; what I want to focus on is tactile feel, and aesthetics and the ability to personalize and create your persona in your keyboard. It's like you're custom building your bike or car; the act alone connects you more with your tools and results in a vibrant and fresh motivation that allows you to invest in your quality of typing. So, touch typing, being fanatic about your home row, learning to use Vim, which results in having Vim everywhere, comes from your ability to appreciate your keyboard which is the thing your hands – which are essentially how you interface your brain with your computer – use all day long.

Either way it won't cost you a lot in time and money and if it all "clicks" (pun intended) for you you'll get an amazing ROI. Today I can type faster than I think, I see the lines and words fly as fast as my eyes can track them, and I probably type faster than I speak.

I feel no barrier between thought and typed text or code. I'm a keyboard fanatic – my first obsession with keyboards was almost

20 years ago around 2000 when I saw a small and efficient keyboard in one of the radar systems I was tasked with during my Army service. It was a Cherry keyboard (same company that makes the Cherry MX mechanical switches that quality mech keyboards use today). Since then keyboards were something I was very interested in for the sake of cutting down the burden of this clumsy interface between a brain and a computer. Took me a while to get to zen. You can start too, just go at it: you can start with a Filco TKL keyboard and MX Brown switches (Google will help you with this).

Keep Opportunities Flowing

Keep a list of opportunities. From a business point of view, these can be ideas for products, possible clients, or ways for people to connect to that can improve your business. From a personal point of view, for example you might have an awesome talk to give, but no takers even though a couple months ago people wanted you to take a spot in a conference but you had no material to talk about.

- Here's an example for the business side. If you don't know how to get your idea out to people, a trick from Lean Startup is to build a website that shows your solution to the fullest extent (think Kickstarter), and now this problem is a funnel problem
- On the personal side, for example you can keep a list of people you know and what in general they can help you with; or, the opposite list of opportunities you need, and people that might be able to help with that. For each meeting that you have, go over that list and see if the person you are meeting with can help bridge you to the opportunity
- Since we're in a world where it's not fun to just get help, but also fun to give back, do the opposite: keep a list of people you can help, and offer them help actively in specific areas that

you know you're valuable for (most times offering a generic, umbrella-like "help", is as good as not offering at all – offer help in something specific)

Either way, find the 2-3 items you can work on that will keep opportunities flowing and embed these into your ways of working.

Build and Maintain Your Network

This one I fail on constantly and still have room to improve, but that doesn't stop me from trying to nail down a formula that would work. It goes like this: spend 30% of your time talking to people, and finding opportunities. What will *actually* happen is that you'll aim for 30% but end up spending 20% of your time doing this, which is a good 80/20 rule.

This is hard because there's always a feeling of having little productivity for just meeting people for coffee. However you're investing in the unknown, which is a different but legitimate kind of *exploration* – keep that in mind. The power of network and opportunity is strong, especially since everyone is doing this, and since everyone is doing this it becomes a market, and since it becomes a market, then probably, somewhere in there – based on my humble knowledge of game theory – you have a currency and value.

One secret to this game is that, well, people *want* to connect you to other people because it makes *them* more valuable, and they may already hold tremendous value because they already invested massive amounts of time (of which a good amount went to waste) just by having coffee with people, and getting to know people, knowing you can't hurry or rush getting to know people. They ended up with what we now understand to be hard earned knowledge of who to connect to whom.

But what happens if these people don't even know you exist? that's what you want to fix and that's what would be worthwhile to invest in. Again, make the important things a habit.

Regularly check-in with close friends; when you're busy creating and building it's easy to neglect your friends. Every two weeks is good enough; but offer more than smalltalk. Beer, lunch and such is a good thing. Set up a bi-weekly calendar alert to do this, with the names of your friends in it. Hey, sales people have all this figured out with CRMs (Customer Relationship Management) systems, they know that these systems make sure to ping them just at the right time to wake up a relationship with someone, and it helps the occasional sales person to remember all your kids' names and what they ate last time you spoke.

I've tried to use a small SaaS CRM for managing my relationships, because why not?, but at some point in time I ditched this idea because I had too many tools, I think to myself – maybe it's time to try again.

When You Can't Start Anything

When you can't start working on anything, no matter the reason: too little time, mood, energy, not in front of the computer, or just not the right timing – you can always break down tasks. Doesn't matter what tasks; wherever you keep them, go over the list and see how you can break those down.

Take a mental hammer and a chisel, and break a task into two smaller tasks, or make it a clearer and more obvious task. Most of the time this requires less brain power than you'd expect, and it feels like you've made it a little more possible for yourself to be successful tomorrow.

Make sure your tasks are easily accessible and available – for me it means it has to be stored on a mobile app. For example, JIRA has a fantastic app and so do most other productivity apps. I break tasks while brushing my teeth or my favorite – standing in line for a cashier, think of it as investing a little energy here and there when you're down, but win more chance for springing back to action the next day when your mood is right, or you have more time, or things just work out to be better for you to start working.

Note: when I say break down tasks – I probably mean anything that grooms a task and makes it more approachable. It can be labeling a task that you've forgotten to label, setting story points when it's missing and more. It also includes pushing and pulling tasks away and into other sprints.

Burn Out

I once read an interesting definition for burn out. It was defined as the *feeling* of investing effort, but nothing gets done (and I might add a *feeling* of "everything is wrong"). For myself, every time I had a burn out, I had gut-feelings and intuition that were plain wrong; because after some rest, and some break, everything made sense again. Only *then* I realized I was going through burn out: so it's a lot about <u>feelings</u> and not facts.

I found that detecting burnout is *very* tricky. Leaving aside *why* burn out happens, and the medical aspects of it since, well, I'm not a doctor, and this is not medical advice, here are some tricks I've used to detect that I'm burning out for myself:

Key indicators:

- Investing a lot of time into something but feeling that everything I do is wrong and that there's generally no good solution in anything I try
- Investing time but having a *feeling* of no progress (focus on the *feeling*)

- Buying lots of stuff. This is a good indicator to notice closely. Some of our buying comes from our insecurity – we buy new stuff to feel better, to hold on to the belief it'll help something, to open a door to *something* new because we feel, figuratively speaking, that all doors are closed, or to keep our minds busy with something completely unrelated and anxiety-free, like a new telescope. Hey, now you know what commercials on TV are trying to do :)

And of course, it always helps to have someone in the room to check yourself against. If you're running solo, bootstrapping a business idea that's pretty hard to do, but in this case having friends or a spouse helps.

Flow Drain

This one actually results *because* you found out how to work effectively. Guess what happens after you:

1. Found your flow
2. Become super productive
3. Happiness levels skyrocket
4. ...You're executing like a machine
5. Quickly draining up work for the current sprint
6. Sprint done! wow that was great!

Well, basically:

1. A growing worry for what to do next. This might start as you're about to finish up your current sprint, and you might procrastinate a lot towards the end
2. Worry about not having the same kind of flow next time. So you don't want this to end and are afraid of "flow breakup"

3. Small pockets of confusion as to what to do next

We solve this by making sure very relevant, very exciting, or simple get-in-get-out tasks make it from the current sprint to the next sprint – they serve as a landing zone into the next sprint. This way you know you have something very relevant, very "atomic" to do already, and you're not spending time "breaking up" with your previous, fantastic flow.

Next, make sure that the next sprint doesn't end up as a bunch of tasks you didn't have time for, or things you didn't really want to do.

So:

1. Have attractive/exciting tasks reassigned from the current sprint to the next one to serve as a landing zone and bridge your "flow"
2. Perform a retro (retrospective, a process for self-reflection). Make sure you know how the retro goes – prepare a checklist and put a task in the current sprint for a retro with simply the same checklist. This task will be in every sprint so just copy/paste it. Retros should get you excited and focused on the next goal. Here's a short checklist for a retro:

Reflect:

- 3 things that went well
- 3 things that went badly
- what goals were advanced the most
- what held you back from executing the most
- what goals were not advanced as they should
- 3 ideas to improve workflow

Act:

- Pick 1 item to improve + schedule to current sprint
- Pick 1 item to serve as workflow optimization + schedule current sprint
- Pick 1 item to help unblocking
- Prioritize one task from a goal that was starved
- Declare the goal for the next sprint in one sentence and name the sprint according to that

Plan:

- Go over backlog, notes, generate new tasks into backlog
- Cherry pick from backlog into sprint, move sprint items that are irrelevant (but gathered during the previous sprint) out of the sprint
- Pick retrospective items
- Prioritize based on goals, make sure all prioritized items are: actionable (for example the title is literally the first action you need to perform in this task - instead of "build reporter infrastructure" start with "add new reporter abstract class"), time estimates are in, epic created and linked, severity and impact filled
- 2-3 iterations to break down tasks (this should take time), make sure all description have all needed materials, links, research material – if extensive research is needed to break the task into research and execution
- Make sure you have two of the special categories picked: E&E

3. Start immediately. Pick a task and perform the first 10 minutes of it. Break.
4. Your new sprint should be hot to enter, without "flow blues".

Low Energy

How effective you are with your work and tasks depends on your mental state. Ever wake up for an alert being on-call and tried to troubleshoot an incident? It's one of those memories that tend to stick. Can you think clearly and take on "heavy" tasks when you're feeling under the weather? Do you feel like making an impact on the world when you're plain tired?

On the flip side, there are many situations in which you want to tear up the world. You just got great feedback on a product you're building, people shared your article and gave you great feedback: "keep on writing!", or you've got lots of hours of sleep and feel super energized, or you just finished a fantastic workout at the gym.

Understanding these mental states which have a close relationship to "effectiveness states", and being aware of them is hard. You might be just starting to get a cold, not noticing it, and hitting a brick wall with an algorithm you're developing and you have no idea why something trivial became so complex to you at that moment. You can't understand why nothing is working, you're quirky, angry, and frustrated – and it doesn't help.

If there were just one mental state that you can train yourself to identify and be aware of, I'd say that would be – identify the times when you have low amounts of energy. When you have low amounts of energy, all you need to do is pick a different kind of task. This also means you want to classify a special category of tasks as "low energy" (you can use a label or what have you). Things like "tidy up my drawers", or "order groceries" or "call the cable company" are useful, but obviously you don't want to use your premium high-energy time for these kind of tasks. Use the "low quality" time where you have low energy.

This also means we discovered a principle: time is not of constant and equal quality. Or in other words an hour isn't always an hour.

As for the rest of the various ups and downs of our effectiveness states – being sick, being moody, and so on, it's very helpful to be able to understand and listen to your body (look up: mindfulness), but I have to say there's very little you can actually *do* at that moment to be mark yourself "effective". When you're sick you need to rest, as the doctor ordered.

The Circadian Rhythm

There are some things that are common to all of us, in theory. In theory, we all should be following the Circadian Rhythm[5] to varying degrees. This means that as humans our bodies and minds were programmed, like all animals, around a cycle that's rooted in our sleep and waking time. The Circadian Rhythm tells us, for example that we're at our highest alertness at 10am. Guess what we're all doing at 10am? that's right. Stand up meetings. What a waste.

A clever manager will move stand up meetings to 14:30pm, where we have "best coordination". But that's not the end of the story; I believe this rhythm is just a starting point, as we're all also affected by things that are new to the world (relatively speaking) such as flights, substances we consume (caffeine, alcohol), and things like blue light from screens which trick our minds about the conditions outside (light vs darkness) and mess with our sleep cycle. The core idea is that you're human: listen to yourself, and try to come up with a way to measure how *you* react to the Circadian Rhythm.

For example, everyone says going to the Gym first thing in the morning is the best. I get absolutely dizzy, low energy, bad gym sessions in the mornings. However I'm completely pumped for planning and prioritization work first thing in the morning. So instead, I use mornings to plan and work; nights for sports and

---

[5]https://en.wikipedia.org/wiki/Circadian_rhythm

gym. Just to note that it took me a few years to accept this as my routine, since everyone kept telling me Gym in the morning is the best; this way I learned there's no "best" when it comes to *your* fitness habits, there's only *you* and the ways you have to measure if things are going well for you.

Know How to Stop

Here's a trick I use often when I write code. Contrary to what people might expect, I stop my work and make an effort to break my code. Sometimes I just either write out – right there and there – in plain english on *code* – what I need to do to continue such as "make sure to reimplement the file reader" which spits out a ton of compiler errors, or the more civilized version of this: write a failing test.

The idea is that the next morning or evening when I open up my project to continue, I start in a "hot seat". I have something that I have to fix immediately in order to start working. Often the act of fixing this *simple* broken code puts me in the right mental state, which is where I stopped the evening or morning before.

So the idea is to leave yourself some mental breadcrumbs. In code it is: break your build in a simple way, you don't want something fancy because you don't want to be stuck *really* figuring out how to fix a broken build.

There's just one problem – if you're going away for a long time, say more than a couple of days from this project, make sure you do the complete opposite. Tidy up everything that you can, make sure the project is in pristine condition before you leave it; you can't afford coming back to a broken project when you're completely out of context because you've been away for a week or two.

I usually tidy up everything and maintain what I call a "work log" on Evernote where I just scribble the day's happenings, like an informal journal, in a tone that sounds like speaking to a friend.

This is an investment – it takes energy to maintain this kind of log so I only do that when I know that I'm context switching between projects for an interval of weeks or a good number of days. A couple weeks later I can read this log and rebound to a great amount of detail.

Commitment Anxiety

Guess what happens when you have everything planned out? Well, you still haven't solved the problem of finding more time, you just have things planned out.

Sometimes when you do your homework right and you plan everything to the letter, you rediscover that time is scarce. You have your 3 hours every evening, and you have your roadmap all laid out, but you find out that you have a task that you've estimated to be 1.5 hours – but you never get to it.

You're not sure if you can lift that kind of a heavy weight; and that investing 1.5 hours – half of your evening time in one bulk is going to give you the feeling you're looking for: "I did a lot today". Some times approaching this task is just a form of anxiety because it's complicated or because it's a lot to do. I call this task commitment anxiety.

This commitment anxiety is fueled by two factors: realizing you're committing a good chunk of your allotment of time, naturally we stay away from this because we feel that we're "paying" a lot of time into just one thing. The second factor is just our natural tendency to conserve energy, we try to keep a balance of not spending energy (which is why we procrastinate).

Here's how I break this anxiety: take a nibble. For every task that weights above an hour, if you have a time window that allows for starting it – start just 10 minutes of work out of this task. After ten minutes, one of two things will happen:

1. You'll just be pulled in and execute this task, overcoming commitment anxiety, or 2. You're going to realize this task needs to be split into two or more subtasks, the first part being "research" or "POC" and the second part being just the boring and dirty work of building something that's already spelled out to the letter.

Basically, *you want to take away choices*, which means your commitment anxiety was simply pronouncing the risk in a task – something that you're not aware of but deep inside you *know* a task contains a good deal of unknowns and your brain wants to stay away from it to avoid failure or the unexpected. You can make the 10 minutes "nibble" work for you while you commute in the morning, before sleep or at another casual point in your day so that it's no big deal to start.

As long as you understand the mechanics of this kind of "anxiety", you might come up with a different technique to "jumpstart" it. The principle is this: you need to learn how to start things which feels uncomfortable starting. Be great at starting, the rest will follow.

Pen and Paper

You might need to tame your mood, focus, energy and "activate" execution mode when "you don't feel like it". I often do that with pen and paper. For example, even if you have a sprint planned out with clear tasks and clear starting points you might still need a "kick in the behind" to commit to pushing goals yourself.

By using pen and paper and spelling out the tasks you want to get done *today* as a to-do list, your brain disconnects from who you are right now, and connects with your primal, younger self. Most of us (I guess it depends on the education system) were taught to use paper and pen in our early life; it makes our brain switch to "action mode" because that's what we were taught as kids: complete a task! – color this image; pencil in the result; underline the odd shape.

Our childhood creates the strongest connections, and we can use it to our advantage.

By the way, sometimes I don't even follow the list I've scribbled down on my desk-side notebook. Sometimes it's just a nice energizer to start focusing but nothing more. Regardless, if I do finish a task that's on a paper list I do cross it out it gives me this great old school feeling of accomplishment. Of course, in any case, I go back to proper task management systems like JIRA, input the time I've spent, and move to "Done" for the relevant tasks for good timekeeping and maintainership.

Control Imbalance

If you want to belong to an upper percentile, to be an overachiever, to be better than anyone else – it means to live in imbalance for some amount of time. By logic, having balance means you're averaging the extremes. If you want to go above average, well, you need to pick an extreme for a while. I'm not talking about dismissing work-life balance, on the opposite, a work-life balance should be a guiding principle because it makes you ultimately more effective. Having *found* work-life balance means you're already above average.

One example of taking myself out of the average, is that I'm not comfortable in services where I get pushed things to me such as programmed TV. I get content as *they* see fit, for whatever definition of "they". To counter this, I consume content in a pull-based fashion so that I could control and moderate it. Nor do I read newspapers. For both of those I set up a personalized way to pull – video and news. That is an *above average* way to consume entertainment and news.

At some point in time I also gave up breakfast with my kids because I felt it breaks my morning "flow" and that I can't spring into action if I have it every morning. Since then I found a middle ground of having just coffee and goofing around with my kids before they go to kindergarten.

There's the old saying where to gain something you have to give up something in return right?. Well, all I'm saying is that you should be aware of that, understand that to go above average has a price, it creates an imbalance, analyze this imbalance, learn how to control it, and live with what you can't control.

Work Full Screen

Here's a trick that sounds silly. When you're working, in a browser, code editor, audio editing software, or whatever – maximize the window and work full screen. If you need multiple windows at the same time (such as reading documentation on the browser while coding), use two physical monitors, one per window.

It works like magic when you step away from your computer and come back. When you come back you don't see an array of options waiting for your attention, you see just one thing – the thing you were doing before you stepped out.

I called it silly because for an outsider it looks like you're limiting what an advanced operating system gives you. Well, here's another trick – a *tiling window manager*. Such a window manager (the thing in the operating system responsible of window layout, arrangement, and more) keeps everything on the screen and it will tile windows on a single plain surface. This means that you can't have too many windows (unless you have a large screen and resolution to accommodate) but it also means that you get the same "full screen" experience because everything you care about is in front of you.

There's no visual context switching other than moving your eyes a few inches here and there. And tiling window managers, are, well, perceived as the tools of kernel hackers and Unix gurus, which is a fun way to think about it.

Oh and did I already say invest in screens?. Big screens. Many screens. There's no point struggling for real-estate when the prices of premium IPS panels these days are very affordable (IPS used to be in the high end category made for graphic and print designers, oh man, do I remember those days).

Turns out if you limit your operating system a little, and make a single physical screen a single window you make your PC a workstation like the old days. Maybe it doesn't only *feel* like the 90's were more productive than today :)

Workflow

If I had to put the workflow I'm suggesting in this book in one sentence it will be something like *GTD meets Scrum meets real life.* To put it in many more sentences, we have to first review some existing methodologies in more depth.

Just Enough Tasks

For lack of a better name I call the first model *Just Enough Tasks.* In this model, we have things to do and we write those down. We might use pen-and-paper or Keep, or Trello, or Asana in a way that models a task list on paper and we'll go ahead and prioritize and maybe set a reminder on some tasks. This is great for small amounts of tasks, and for an environment with a good time margin for error. For example, grocery lists are in this category. With grocery lists if you forget an item, that's OK (hopefully), and there aren't *too many* items on that list because after all it's limited by what you can carry or what you can store. It's also a one-time effort; you don't go to the store multiple separate times over the week, you probably prefer going there just once. You might also use this for small-scale projects and errands.

The downsides of this model follow from the description: it's a low scale, low risk and a low time-stress model. You don't want to model building a house with a simplistic task list because of the implications of making a mistake. You don't want to plan a software project for a client with a simple task list because of the implication of not understanding your delivery and velocity (in other words: "will I make it in time?") and the fact that you're contractually obligated to a timeline.

GTD

Getting Things Done, or: GTD, is a time management method described in the book of the same title by David Allen. It is one approach to productivity that made a *significant* dent in how I think and work and so I strongly recommend getting the book or reading the shorter "GTD in 15 minutes"[6]. I can't count how many times I've sent people this link and followed closely to help them implement GTD in their professional life and it changed at least how they think not to mention how they work for the better.

After around four to five years practicing GTD to the letter I discovered that it lacked in a few areas, and by the way, some of these were by-design because GTD is designed to be technology agnostic leaving some important questions unanswered:

- What tools to use and how to set them up so that I get a great user-experience through desktop, mobile and so on?
- What to do when I'm out of time? or out of time to plan?
- How to plan and execute on *software*?
- How to connect GTD with goal making? There's a brief about that in the book, but it's not as elaborate as a full on methodology such as OKR (Objectives and Key Results) so that I can systemize it.
- How to deal with the flaws that exists in *me* or how I run my life? How to take advantage of my strengths and skip over my weaknesses?

Waterfall, Scrum, Agile, Kanban

There are many methodologies to produce software that we've seen in the past 30 years. Namely: waterfall, Scrum, Kanban, and

---

[6]https://hamberg.no/gtd/

maybe the "higher level" Agile movement. I'll tell you a little secret – at large, they all work. There are so many variables that get overlooked when they fail that make people have blind moves from one methodology to another that create a reality where at any given time you'll have a negative overview of one methodology and a negative of the other.

The daring truth is simple: apply the right solution to the problem at hand.

I too was a big fan of Agile when it all started. I was working with engineers from Finland, Denmark, and I've got to experience first-hand from kind of where it all started; I was exposed to the core truths of Agile, without all the marketing buzz. I found out something simple: "This is how it works, and it works for us.".

It works for us. That's something that a marketer will never use. You can't market Agile courses, consultants, and by-products if you say "Hey, it works for us, maybe it'll work for you".

For self productivity and effective work I found out the following:

1. As in software, waterfall is too big and too slow to iterate on as an individual (but again there *are* situations where waterfall is still perfect)
2. Kanban is destructive for motivation. While it *looks like* Kanban is perfect for the individual; the tempting "execute as much as you can and just-in-time", it creates a mess. Soon your board is full, your lists are cluttered, your motivation and focus is destroyed. You can't be a factory worker – in Software – and be self-motivated at the same time. I'm lucky to have worked on a suite of software products for optimizing production floors such as Foxconn's and Nokia's – I got to see Kanban in factories, in its natural habitat, in real life, and it was amazing; there was a huge cultural side to support Kanban that is completely missing in Software and is too nuanced to teach a software team leader because it's not

part of the day to day, and you don't study production in universities (maybe that's too bad). For example; you don't get to *see* a chip-shooter stop working because it's missing a feeding belt of components because it wasn't on the Kanban board, and then the clock-work of teamwork for fixing this, and then see how the way the hierarchy of *learning* at the factory works. A chat with the production floor manager was *always* on systems theory and queues and Kanban – you could talk for days about Kanban. Again, for better or worse, this is not the focus in software production; we're suckers for buzzwords because it costs nothing to adopt and it costs nothing to waste if we made a mistake. The cost of change in a production floor is *physically* hard, as well as very expensive. The cost of waste in a production floor is, well, as one production floor manager told me: "If I get just two hours of downtime in a year because a bug in your software, that would cost the factory the same as the license you sold me; so you can't fail", and the license we sold was in the range of millions of dollars a year per such customer.

After fighting hard for a few years, I realized Kanban was bad for me. I then turned into Scrum to facilitate sprints; I found that high focus, concentrated productivity periods and the sense of success with each of those coming to completion created a system that can hold focus and motivation effectively as well as give place to improve and fine tune without breaking that focus.

In a sense, if a sprint is two weeks, I'm committing to it on the expense that I'm making a mistake in direction, but I'm not risking my motivation and focus. With Kanban, I was challenging my direction every few tasks; for all the savings I had in little "waste" I paid in focus and self-motivation.

When you think about it, after practicing GTD to the letter for a long period of time – the line between Kanban and GTD also becomes blurred; so you might find out that GTD without a supportive framework has the same dynamic as Kanban when looking at motivation and focus. In that regard, if you choose to adopt GTD, you *can* change it to suit you and that's OK.

OKR

OKR[7] or "Objectives, Key Results" is a framework for defining and tracking objectives and their outcomes. Put simply in my words, it's a way to track high-level to low level objectives in a big organization when you have many people, many opinions that create a communication network that's hard to grasp.

With OKR and the tooling that support it you set a hierarchical goal level from "Smooth payments" down to "Have a mobile payments app" to "Have a secure user experience on mobile" and finally down to "Use iOS keychain and secure enclave for private user details". Where each of these have their key results and progress and are tracked in an aggregative fashion as you go up the stack.

While there are a few more details to this methodology, such as setting over-achieving goals and ways to present progress and communication, what I just described is the gist of it.

Purpose-Goals-Tasks = GTD + Scrum + OKR

This is what I ended up with. Lacking a cool name, I've called my workflow *Purpose-goals-tasks* and designed it so that it takes principles from GTD for its sense of pragmatism and setting up the mind for success, Scrum for execution and its iterative nature, and lastly a variant of OKR (Objectives Key Results) for motivation, focus, and goal setting.

---

[7]https://en.wikipedia.org/wiki/OKR

I am not affiliated with JIRA, I used it as well as Pivotal Tracker and YouTrack and others it in my workplaces for varying degrees of success.

A couple years ago I was running out of tools (I tried Pivotal Tracker, Trello, Asana and others) that can do what I wanted – for personal productivity. I decided to make a personal JIRA account where I can go wild. I found that with the liberty of making up my own scheme on top of JIRA I was able to make it do everything I ever wanted and so I've become a fan.

Workflow Applied: JIRA

Let's see how JIRA can be used as a powerful workflow daily driver. We're going to say this: JIRA can be a tool to drive a hybrid workflow between just-enough GTD, a full blown task manager, just-enough OKR (objective management), and an implementation of my custom purpose-goals-tasks framework with all the nuances we've highlighted.

First let's set up our abstractions or in other words: terminology.

1. **Purpose**. A purpose is your 5-10 year life achievement goal. This is "stored" in your own private lists, not in JIRA. It's your sense of purpose. If you like, you can actually model it as a meta-epic in JIRA but it serves no mechanical purpose in your day to day workflow.
2. **Goal**. A goal is an Epic in JIRA. Use the **Classic** JIRA, not the new-gen, then select **Scrum** and not kanban. If your 5 year purpose is to be a data scientist then one goal, modeled as an epic, can be to complete the Coursera Machine Learning course while another goal that's modeled as an epic could be to deliver a machine learning project for your first client.
3. **Task**. A task is a JIRA story. We also have JIRA bugs, tasks and so on but let's leave those as placeholders if we have

any other abstraction to model in the future. For now, a Task is a JIRA story. Each task must be: prioritized (select priority), gauged for impact (this is a measurement of ROI – we're taking the **positive** Impact on business meaning here, as opposed to the original meaning of negative impact or "damage"), estimated for story points (in hours), and when finished, we must put back time spent on the task with Time Tracking feature/field. Optionally we can use labels to say things about what it requires from our mood (energetic), or our physical location (pharmacy) just like in GTD.

Here's what it looks like:

STATUS

Selected for Development ˅

PRIORITY

↑   Highest

IMPACT

4 - Extensive / Widespread

STORY POINTS

1

TIME TRACKING

   No time logged

COMPONENTS

None

LABELS

None

SPRINT

Sprint2: Spectral Sales + Deps

EPIC LINK

Spectral

And a breakdown:

- **Description**. Actionable description, you should be reading this and have everything you need to start. If you read this and say "well, I'm not sure about X", then you should work some more on grooming this task.
- **Priority**. This is how you think this item is prioritized; you're putting on the Product hat and making a decision based on what you know about the world.
- **Impact**. Originally this was made to gauge a bug or issue impact on your clients. Here we want to gauge positive impact on your business. There *are* low-priority items in your product that make a huge impact – how about writing a blog post about fake news perfectly timed when there's a huge controversy around?
- **Story points**. This is your time unit. I keep it as hours.
- **Time tracking**. I feed back time spent on every finished task. Since there's no one managing you or watching your back this is probably the only way to keep yourself honest and compare against estimated Story Points.
- **Components**. As in software, modules in your subsystem. With this you can later track "complex" parts or problematic parts in what you're building.
- **Labels**. This is for general use. I typically use it for the classic GTD context; labels such as "@doctor" means I have a low-wifi environment, and probably around 40min of waiting time. If I happen to be at the doctor's office, I can filter for this tag and have my next ideal task served to me.
- **Sprint** and **Epic Link** are populated for you by JIRA when you associate tasks with an epic or sprint (or by you if you want to override things).

4. **Sprint**. Similar to a Sprint in JIRA. We cherry-pick items from our backlog, and place them on something we've "committed"

to execute, a sprint. While in Scrum a sprint is used to help synchronize an organization, here it's primarily used to channel learning, focus and motivation and not at all to synchronize anything.

5. **Incoming.** This is a GTD concept and we map it to a Backlog in JIRA. We place incoming and 'next' items from the GTD workflow into our JIRA project backlog, with basic prioritization. When we finish a sprint, we create another sprint and cherry-pick from our backlog the set of new tasks we want to commit to and focus on for the next week or so (you decide how long is a sprint).

6. **Priority.** We prioritize with a combination of what you would expect in software plus what you would expect from GTD. For example, we want to prioritize items that are important, but also that are small and easy to pick when you just happen to have the spare time. Here's one example (JQL): `project = MYPRJOECT ORDER BY priority DESC, Impact DESC, cf[10016] ASC, cf[10026] ASC, labels ASC, created DESC, rank ASC` (the cfXXX part are story points). So in principle: priority, impact, story points, and so on. We want to first tackle the tasks that are: important and have high impact, and also are easy to execute. Your sprint will be sorted this way and your backlog will be sorted this way. You're getting high ROI by default all the time.

Now let's talk about what we've created by saying what kind of **abilities** we unlock with this model for free just by using what JIRA presents, in no particular order.

1. Understand how much work we're facing for this week, by looking at the Sprint points

2. Ability to filter and view only items relating to a certain goal (which is an Epic, remember?). This is helpful if we feel like we want to create a single block of tasks for just one project instead of context switching; or if we want to cancel

all together all of those tasks. We can also "feel" how much we're investing in for this week, and which projects we're not investing in as much as we need for this week. Just a glimpse of colors, which JIRA gives you for free can give you a good feeling of how you're balancing the "push" on all of your goals for this week. Note every time I say 'week' I mean Sprint and vice versa; so you might pick two weeks or a month as your Sprint cadence interval

3. Ability to filter by mood, location and other tags that indicate context, by playing with labels, this enables GTD's contextual aspects

4. Ability to see which task fits the time you currently have by looking at story points. If you go and make a half an hour of focus time, because that's only what you have today, go and pick a tasks for 0.5 worth of points. It lets you be honest with the time you have and the amount of effort you can spend.

5. Create focus by drafting a Sprint, cherry pick only the important stuff and commit your focus for a week. You see how your goals interplay with your sprint which interplay with your tasks immediately, and so you can see how you're moving your goals with the help of the sprint you're drafting (this is doing OKR in a sense)

6. Visualize the amount of work per goal (JIRA gives you this for free, because these are epics)

7. Create dependencies between goals (again, this is standard work with Epics)

8. Use any JIRA productivity and optimization data-driven approaches like standard burndown charts, pie charts, custom reports and so on.

9. Model task dependencies (just standard JIRA task dependencies)

10. Ability to defer something you're not ready for that just entered the backlog to the next sprint, while working on Sprint 1, you can participate in semi-planning of Sprint 2 already by placing the important issues you know you want

to work on but can't have the focus right now to shuffle and don't want to forget about.

Workflow:

1. Ongoing: tasks go into backlog (following GTD for small tasks: if you can perform the task in 2 minutes go do it and don't bother putting in backlog), are labeled, filed, marked priority impact and points. Or if you already practice GTD in Evernote or other kind of system, when tasks mature from your already-existing "fast GTD" workflow into something you really need to do.
2. Sprint planning: when a sprint finishes or on a cadence. Go over backlog, and cherry-pick items according to a good mixture of driving your goals.
3. Execution: every day pick and choose what you want to execute based on focus, energy and context (the GTD context). You can context-switch for having more interesting time or divide the sprint and take on work only from a couple goals. To support a data driven workflow, when finishing a task, set back how long it took (using JIRA's built in time tracker). Take this opportunity to also break down tasks you think are too big, keep the pieces in the same sprint or move them to the next – this is how you maintain focus.
4. Sprint closing: make sure time spent is fed back into every task, in general you also want to confirm tasks are labeled, estimated, and are in pristine condition before parting ways with those. File a note for sprint retro: 3 things that worked well, 3 that didn't, and extract one action item for next time into the next sprint, regardless of its priority and impact.

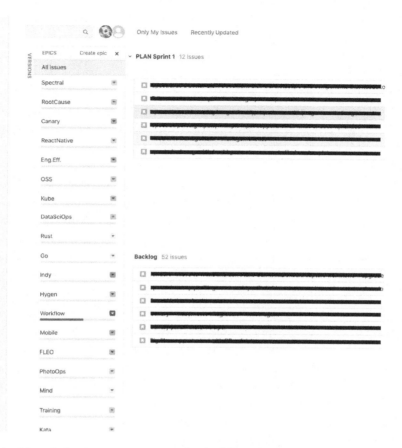

And here's how an issue screen looks like, where the most important fields for our purpose are on top:

Issue layout

PARA: Scrum Default Issue Screen

Choose fields to show and set their order for the below issue types in Paracode Workflow. To make more fields available, or to add and edit field tabs, go to PARA: Scrum Default Issue Screen.

☑ Task   ▦ Sub-task   ▢ Story   ⊡ Epic

DESCRIPTION AREA   What's this?

≡ Description

PRIMARY FIELDS   What's this?

⇅ Priority

◉ Impact

▦ Story Points

⏱ Time tracking

≔ Components

🏷 Labels

🗂 Sprint

≔ Epic Link

SECONDARY FIELDS   What's this?

④ Assignee

④ Reporter

⌘ Releases panel

⌥ Development

Workflow Applied: Evernote

I used Evernote to capture "soft" items such as general thoughts, product ideas and research, sales ideas, and other general notes. I apply GTD[8] in here too, and once in a while I graduate certain tasks from evernote into the JIRA backlog or sprint plan. If you don't already have such a system for your notes, then you might want to start with JIRA so that such a need "naturally" arise.

---

[8]https://hamberg.no/gtd/

- ▾ ⭐ Shortcuts
  - ▢ Inbox 32
  - ▢ Icebox 16
  - ▢ Tickler 1
  - ▢ Waiting for 8
  - ▢ ---------
  - ▢ Now 49
  - ▾ ☰ Next
    - ▢ Batch 18
    - ▢ Booksh... 6
    - ▢ Coderev 10
    - ▢ Practice 8
    - ▢ Read 60
    - ▢ Tasks 6
    - ▢ Watch 10
    - ▢ Write 19
  - ▾ ☰ Projects
    - ▢ Engine... 5

Workflow Applied: Make It Stick

There's a good chance you'll read, agree, and understand everything that's been said here. That, and struggle with having time to force yourself to plan, feed back data, maintain the world of knowledge, goals, tasks, and efficiency around you. Or in short – you'll struggle in making yourself productive because you aren't being productive with planning; the chicken and the egg problem.

There are a couple ways to do this. One is being persistent, being honest when you fail and getting back on the horse. Keep this in mind – when you're feeling the system doesn't work, you are probably planning wrong, make sure you force yourself to re-evaluate, schedule and actually follow through to proper planning and following your workflow.

The second way to do this is to treat your efficient workflow as a ceremony. As some kind of a religious act, something sacred. Look around you, religion works because practitioners (also called "followers") follow a very strict form of framework, sometimes demanding, and I'm pretty sure it's demanding of their private time – because they believe that believing is something above everything else. If you treat your planning time as somewhat sacred, give it some kind of higher-kinded value (I leave this to you), then maybe you won't need to *force* yourself to follow system; it'll come naturally. Need ideas for this? well, for starters, you need values.

The effective workflow values.

- *Time and your use of time is sacred.* We all have a very limited window of time to make an impact; make it count.
- *Go above and beyond.* Treat challenges with respect – plan out the risks and blockers. Break it down into digestible tasks. Make every task lead to the next. Have a plan B. Make solving challenges and execution a form of art.

- *Be a craftsperson.* If you choose to do something, have proper values baked into it. Invest significant amount of time in building it right. Perform above the standard. Be proud of your work. Don't chase perfection for the sake of perfection because that would be a fool's errand; if you have a principle of "good is better than perfect" be proud of that. Put it on posters in your home office. I have posters of the original LEGO and Phillips screw patent filings on my wall and it inspires me: two inventions that are painfully simple yet strikingly amazing.

Plan Actively for Tomorrow

If you're executing today, it's too hard to also plan a perfect tomorrow. I mean literally tomorrow. And thinking about the next day at the end of the current day isn't that great of a use of your depleted reserves of focus. In the context of a sprint, you should have an idea of what you want to do tomorrow but you probably don't actively nail it down to the letter.

What sometimes happens is that you're approaching the next day the next morning trying to figure out where you left off or what would be the best thing to do from the barrage of options you have – classical *paradox of options*. To unblock this, while doing your nightly ceremonies make sure you pick just *one* task or goal you want to get done tomorrow from what you know you should be doing for the sprint. This is what you should keep in mind before going to sleep and this is what you should have in mind when you wake up.

You are picking just one task. I know, there's a bunch of these already planned and your sprint is laid out – and it's hard to pick just one of the many things that needs to be done. However, odds are you're going to pick the most important, or challenging, or exciting task for tomorrow. The rest of the day will probably either way surround itself around this task. The rest of the tasks are already pretty secondary; so picking just one task is still smart.

Pick this one task, and try to imagine what it takes for it to be successful. If you discover something very important you should remember, go ahead and write a note for yourself but stop there. And if you didn't, at least you've primed your brain for what needs to happen tomorrow and probably still remember this the morning after; which is very important – you want to be focused in the morning on what you want to achieve for the day and what is the most important thing to achieve. Even if you failed, at least you failed fast on the most important experiment you needed to run.

Make this a habit. Think about the one big task for tomorrow each day before sleep for a few minutes. If you're like me you'll need to give yourself a small reminder – write it on a paper note and leave it on your desk, or in your Evernote or just send yourself an email.

Remember. You're reaching for your productivity and have no manager. It's up to you to be your own manager, and if you had a manager, you'd get the weekly or daily focus in your email or a reminder of what's important served to you on a post-it on your table. You're creating this dynamic yourself. Look through your lists and think about tomorrow; then say – "Tomorrow I'm finishing the remaining 1.5 points, and closing the sprint; the most important thing is to close the sprint so I can create a move-forward momentum".

Reflect

Have a process to look back on any of the points here, and assess your performance. If your topic area is inherently measurable (e.g. how long it took to perform a task), then you have it easy. Some areas are hard to measure and you will have to resort to feelings and educated guesses, what's important here is to be completely honest with yourself.

It helps to understand what are human biases and what are the classes of biases so that you don't drill yourself into a hole. If you can have a different person help you as an echo wall that would be great.

It will be worth your time to learn about human biases – take a look at this list[9] from Wikipedia. In addition it's worth knowing about biases in decision making and ways to solve for that, also known as razors[10].

One bias that we probably all have is *Sunk Cost*. We tend to justify losses to ourselves by providing what looks to us as reasonable explanation and we'll make it as elaborate as possible to be valid – instead of stopping short and "cutting our losses". We do this because we feel sorry for having already invested in something, we feel attached to it, we feel part of it. On the flip side, product people will use this to build "sticky" products. Ever wondered why it's hard to switch phones even though it makes complete sense to you that you should?

One famous razor that will make your life easier is Occam's Razor. It states that *simpler explanations are more likely to be correct; avoid unnecessary or improbable assumptions*, and is based on the fact that most things are simple, most people are normative. There's a *normal distribution* to everything in life. However the human mind sometimes likes to give abnormal explanations to things it doesn't understand. When candidates are late to an interview I always treat them with understanding while there are many who would mark that one as "being late for interview equals being late every day at work" which is the most irrational thing to assume – in fact it's completely logical for candidates to be late for an interview. It's a new place, it's a new address, it's between breaks in their current job, and they're juggling to do their best which often leads to the opposite result out of stress. Occam's Razor says: assume the simplest. They're simply late because we're hard to find.

---

[9]https://en.wikipedia.org/wiki/List_of_cognitive_biases
[10]https://en.wikipedia.org/wiki/Philosophical_razor

Regardless of these couple of examples, we put some more focus in this book on popular biases in the *Learning* chapter.

Rituals

Evernote is where I keep my notes. It's my "Product" knowledge-base. JIRA is for tasks and goals and execution. It's my "Engineering" knowledge base. You have to maintain both, and sometimes they'll mirror one another. It will take time and reflection to find your pace and finally agree to pay the price of double maintenance.

Fact is that as a productivity worker you're both a maker and a visionary. It takes significant amounts of time to be both.

Next we're going to look at the "ceremonies" that need to happen in order to do that maintenance. The goal is to always have a correct "next" action to do, just like in GTD; only this time we also want to work on the correct next goal, to invest in the correct purpose in life and keep energy and momentum as with plow through.

Daily Sprint Execution

- Random idea? random raw task?
  * Less than 2m? do it
  * Can't do it? let someone else do it, delegate
  * Can do it? great!

  * Translate into a visible and physical action (maybe the first action that starts the task) + include needed resources in body (articles, videos, emails, names, phone numbers)
  * Put under JIRA backlog, under the relevant epic, if it's a clear epic-based task finish here.
  * If it's a vague, non-epic, non-goal, thinking/planning, soft task put it in Evernote Incoming. If you're promoting Incoming to Next, you want to classify, just like in GTD:

* Workflow: indicate what kind of "next" this is: writing, reading, etc.

* Objective/Project: give it one label based on the project or objective it belongs to, and should "account under"

* Context: give it a context tag such as "#code", if a person use @person-name (and/or @company-name or @place) this helps pull all notes when speaking to someone or in social interactions

* ONLY IF CRITICAL move to 'now'

- If it's morning, perform an E&E task (explore and experiment)
  * It's reasonable that after you explore an idea you end up with a bunch of new ideas or tasks. These go to your Evernote inbox or JIRA backlog respectively
- Otherwise pick a task from the current JIRA sprint and execute
- Stick to these sprint job-stealing/shuffling rules as you browse through the daily work, and around the sprint:
  - If you can't execute, groom – break tasks, tag them, estimate them, prioritize them, or start just 10 minutes out of a certain task.
  - If you're about to finish a sprint, locate a dead-easy task, a "hot" task, and instead of going for the easy target, push it to the next sprint so you have a great 'landing zone' for bridging your productivity from current sprint to the next sprint
  - If you finished a sprint, you should be looking at the retro task now which every sprint should contain: just a task called "retro"; that's all that remains, stop here and rest. Do the retro the next day and make sure you're energetic.
- During mid-day perform your GTD crunch, and sprint crunch
  - In Evernote, sort out your inbox and "now": kill irrelevant tasks, or promote tasks to JIRA backlog

> – In JIRA, go over your backlog: kill irrelevant tasks, break
> tasks into smaller ones, promote tasks into the next
> sprint or demote tasks out of the current sprint

- Scan your calendar for meetings. Meetings are important
  since they break up your productivity and influences your
  sprint execution.
- Scan your Waiting-for and Tickler notebooks in Evernote (for
  Waiting-for and Tickler see here[11])

Why perform your ceremonies *mid-day*? According to a study by
Golder and Macy ("Diurnal and Seasonal Mood Vary with Work,
Sleep, and Daylength Across Diverse Cultures", 2011) your mid-day
should be the low-point and so, it's a bad time for creativity and
getting things done. Not only that, because as the research shows,
people feel more negative or pessimistic, it's the perfect time to
estimate; you'll be naturally pessimistic in your estimations and
that would serve as a counterbalance for the optimism bias (see
more about this in Time Management).

Sprint Closing

Perform a retro. You should have such a task and it is the last one
in the sprint. If not add it. The result of the retro is yet more tasks
into the next sprint and backlog.

List out:

- 3 things that went well
- 3 things that went badly
- what goals were advanced the most
- what held you back from executing the most
- what goals were not advanced as they should
- 3 ideas to improve workflow

---

[11]https://hamberg.no/gtd/

Act:

- Pick 1 item to improve + schedule to current sprint
- Pick 1 item to serve as workflow optimization + schedule current sprint
- Pick 1 item to help unblocking
- Prioritize one task from a goal that was starved
- Declare the goal for the next sprint in one sentence and name the sprint according to that

Sprint Planning

You've finished a sprint retro, and closed the current sprint. You should have various tasks already in the current sprint as:

1. A result of the retro
2. The "landing zone" tasks from the previous sprint. Tasks that are easy, nice, hot, and quick to get into in order to pick up your productivity where you left off before "breaking" to sprint planning

Now we need to take a look at three things:

1. Your list of goals (epics) and priorities. How's that going? what's being held down? what's urgent?
2. Your existing new sprint with a few new tasks in it
3. Your backlog

You want to push in from the backlog or pull out from the sprint tasks that don't contribute to (1), meaning that don't work towards your goal. This is planning the sprint.

Once you're done, you want to iteratively grind down tasks:

1. Make sure all tasks are titled as the first action in the task (actionable)
2. Go over tasks 2-3 times and try to break them down to smaller tasks
3. Make sure all tasks have estimates, impact, priorities, epics, labels and that the description contains all researched material needed. If something doesn't have the material needed and it takes more than a few minutes to complete create a new task named "research" and link it as a precondition
4. Look at the finished task list and do a small negotiation with yourself – is it too much? move off low-priority to a next-next sprint or backlog. Then plan how you execute everything by ordering in what you think will give you the best flow (I guess grouping tasks by projects or matching timeboxes to vacations or weekends)
5. Have one of the special-category E&E (explore and experiment) tasks picked
6. Lastly add a placeholder "retro" task where in the meanwhile you'll gather insights but that you will execute only when the sprint finishes.

That's it, start the sprint:

- Start immediately. Pick a task and perform the first 10 minutes. Break.
- Your new sprint should be hot to enter, without "Flow blues".

Weekly Trigger List

There's a concept of forcing open-loops in GTD. Even with an airtight system like GTD there can be some misses. The idea is that you have a few "keywords" around to provoke things you've missed, forgotten, or set up for later and never come back to. This list is called your "trigger list" and it's completely personal; it's something you build for yourself and grow with you.

Here are a bunch of keywords to get you started:

- Projects
- Boss
- Co-workers
- Projects started, not completed
- Projects that need to be started
- People I need to get back to
- Social events: meetups
- Saying thanks to people
- Go over "burning" Github issues
- Look for new conferences, podcasts sources for gym and running
- Tech news
- Go over book recommendations
- Focus note — what do i want to do in life

Weekly Goal Planning

This can be weekly or every two weeks or maybe months. We want to answer the question: "Are we still on course to our 5-year plan?". We want to answer the bigger question but we'll look at how our goals are doing in practice.

- Go over epics in JIRA, see if you've been investing to reflect your purpose
- Take a step back and think if this is the best ROI you can have, or should you kill a project and swap it with a new one. If possible do this with another person.
- Go over Icebox for surprise items that might become relevant

- Go over backlog see if there's an item to kill or promote (this is always a good idea)
- Go over your ideas folder (assuming you maintain one) to see if there's anything worth promoting as a goal

Goals & Planning

In this chapter, we'll touch some *fuzzy* aspects of prioritization, understanding what's important and what's a goal.

Impact and Delegation

First to consider when thinking about goals and planning is: instead of prioritizing X, can we actually *not* do X at all?

We can:

1. Cancel it. Decide it's not important (cancellation)
2. Let someone else do it! (delegation)
3. Decide to do it later (de-prioritization)

These bear the appropriate questions:

1. Is X making an impact? translate impact into something tangible: money, clicks, traffic. If so, is it enough impact to cross a threshold and classify "needs to be done"?
2. *Can* someone else do X (e.g. are they skilled for it)? *should* someone else do it (e.g. is it cost-effective?). If so, *when* can they do it?
3. Can it be done *later* while still not hurting any of our KPIs, or starving any of our KPIs?

Make a habit of asking yourself these questions and asking others as well. Often times we're interlocked into an execution framework but forget that sometimes delegation works and is more effective (and other times it isn't – but the point is to be able to *consider* it).

Work the Right Things

Within goals that you've already decided that do make an impact, and goals that you've delegated – hides a category of the "right things" to work on. But there's one dimension missing here: time. *Working on the right things* must be expanded to "Working on the right things at the right time". It's often easy to drop that last part.

But how do we classify "right things"? What's right? Here are a few pointers that I use.

- Work on things that return investment in the most efficient way towards the amount of time (or money) that you invest
- Develop a system to measure and optimize your workflow. Find pockets of inefficient execution and understand the "whys".
- Constantly groom goals, projects, tasks to serve as an effective investment. Sometimes problems with returning your time investment is directly connected to unexpected reasons: you might just be tired, and so can't get much out of an hour of work. Or, you've defined the task badly – in the sense that you start it and don't know how to end it. *Definition of done* is one way to help yourself make sense of tasks that you define. This is the practice where you explicitly describe how a task ends, what makes it a success and what defines it as "finished".

Time is scarce, and, surprise, not all time is created equal. When you add *yourself* into the equation, an hour isn't really a wall-clock hour.

If you just won yourself a free evening to work on your idea but you didn't sleep well because of a new baby, or because of any kind of stress, that precious free-evening worth of time isn't the same as a free evening where you are refreshed, energized, motivated.

So, let's analyze, in order to make full use of scarce time you need to:

- Be rested
- Be energetic
- Be motivated: "we're doing this for a *reason*"
- The where: "where" in a figurative speak, it's actually your context. you need to know the next step is compatible with where you are physically, how you feel, and what you *can* do at this point in time.
- The what: have a good idea about what's the next step. Have the next task lined up
- The how: have a good idea how to do it
- The when: and make sure that the how fits the when – that you set yourself for success (i.e. if you only have half an hour don't attempt at a 3-hour worth of tasks)
- Know when you're done – how does success look like (also, partly a motivation piece)

Go Through a Required Self-Observation

Behind these requirements there's an even bigger list of requirements. For example, to be motivated, you need to know that your task is going into something that matters. For your task to be listed under "things that matter" it has to be connected to a "higher" goal. So now, you have to have your list of goals.

For these goals to make sense, you have to understand what you get out of each goal, how to prioritize goals, and when's the best time to act upon a goal. Also, since sometimes in order to be the world's best scientist, you have to start by being the world's modest math student, some goals have prerequirements. Now you have a graph of goals, or a tree of dependent goals to manage. And, finally, these goals have to connect with who you are, and what you think of yourself, and how it helps you to get to who you want to be.

We've converted this list of goals into a list of life-achievements to build for yourself, and that list requires self-introspection and self coaching that's not so easy to do.

Sometimes it can be simple. You can have a goal that says "Build an app to make $40K" and that doesn't need too much self introspection and some higher form of thinking and meaning. It's money and money can be put into many other goals you want to achieve in life.

So the key, like most of us already know, is to be able to set goals. But now we've removed the cliche and soft stuff from that saying, and connected it with something very practical that's razor sharp. In order to make the best use of our time, we have to have tasks lined up, they must have clear definitions, that are very strict or we don't even try picking them up.

There's also some mechanics involved, if we've connected tasks to goals, and we've been prioritizing goals within the goal list and tasks under any goal between their sibling tasks; wouldn't it be nice to approach a bunch of tasks from a goal point of view? for instance, say you just had a goal of "Build a time tracker". However, 6 months into this stint, you discover your best competition is now offering their product for free, breaking your assumption of being in advantage by providing a free time tracker yourself.

You might want to wait a couple months and invest in other goals while you see what happens with your competition and their new offering. Putting all tasks, spread across backlogs, boards, and sprints aside as part of de-prioritizing the time tracker, with a one-click/drag might be extremely useful. In fact, it should be easy to do since you have already created this abstraction in the proper way. I do this exact thing with JIRA (more on this in the Workflow chapter).

Here's a useful checklist of questions to ask yourself for each of your candidate goals.

- Preconditions
    - What do you get out of it?
    - When the goal is complete, what's the reality? Imagine what it feels like
    - What time does it save?
    - What money does it make?
    - Is it a segway into or prerequirement of another goal?
    - What's required to achieve a goal?
    - Can you pay someone to achieve it?
    - Should you accomplish this at all? what are the ways you have to *not* do this goal?
- Priority
    - Why is it important?
    - Is there a time constraint?
    - Is there a market or client opportunity?
    - What's the price or damage estimate of *not* doing it right now?
    - If done right now rather than later, does it help other goals?
- Effort
    - Can it be broken into tasks?
    - Pricing: hours to invest? resources to expense?
- Execution
    - Can you have clear blocks of time, per your custom schedule (constraints like kids, etc.)?
    - Is this goal a context-switch party? Does it depend on other people? other companies?
    - What kind of energy, motivation, and thinking depth it requires?
    - Can it be done casually? (e.g. I'm sitting in the doctor's office, give me something to read)

Have a Purpose

This is a hard one. Assuming you have a perfect list of goals; how do you know everything is executing well? that the ship is sailing the right way. For example if you had just one uber-goal of "Buying a house" or "A trip around the world" and then your actual sub-goals of "Sell software for Mac" are just means to that great end, then if you look at the bank and you have enough money for buying a house, you're done. After 10 years of working hard you're done – you've completed this uber-goal, or *purpose*. Now what? welcome to midlife crisis.

Kidding aside (although the above has a lot of truth in it, actually), within these 10-some years you want to know you are moving in the right direction.

If you have an uber-goal, let's call it maybe a "purpose" then it's a powerful motivational tool. If you don't have it, then you're in a midlife crisis, I guess?. It's OK to not have that as a kid, but as an adult with a family to support, it's probably a very smart idea to sort out your list of "purpose".

Model Product Value

It's very easy to build the wrong thing and even when you know you're building the right thing, its easy to build it wrong.

I love comparing software engineering to traditional engineering industries like construction. Besides stirring up the classic debate of "Is software engineering art or engineering?", the reason I pick construction is because it has critical consequences if you've made a mistake early in the process, it has a big-design-upfront process, and in fact most implications are critical across the board.

Plus, we all know getting a house is one of the bigger expenses in life, and we all hope the best engineers built *our* house, right?

I'll be comparing construction to software engineering. In the same sense where you want to model a building, you want to model your product or more specifically product value.

How can I explain having witnessed so many ways to build products? so many product managers with different approaches? so many different processes to produce the same thing: software?

One way I explain it is that our industry is still young, and it doesn't help that our technology building blocks pretty much change completely every 3-4 years. In addition, since we're dealing with virtual material and virtual waste, it's too easy to convince people of an idea and of a way to build it, while both being wrong.

And every one love to hate product specs right? It's been written off too many times as a time waster, as a blunt instrument, as the non-agile way to build software. Well I'm here to say: "The product spec is dead. Long live the product spec".

First, let me deal with the misconceptions:

1. The reason product specs were written off, is sociological. It turned out product managers were focusing on writing the product spec rather than on writing a spec that will enable a great product.
2. The alternative selected to a product spec is a form of an agile user story.
3. Some times product specs were treated like a blunt checklist.

A product spec has one goal: to model thought. Without further delay, here's how I model product value – it's a template that you can use, with details baked in under each headline.

— snip here —

Spec Title

Goal
The goal state should "set the atmosphere", set the business value in

clear terms, and supply reason for: (1) why do it (2) why now.

Use Cases / Requirements
Supply a structured list of use cases in the typical BDD format: "As a /persona/ I want to be able to /perform goal/ in order to /business value/". In many cases this can be a table, linking a user story to a JIRA epic (use any other issue tracker you like).

Assumptions
Supply a list of hypothesis or assumptions. We want to be able to list everything we know about the world that can explain why we wrote this spec the way we wrote it. The goal here is, given a mistake, to be able to correct it quickly.

Solutions Considered
Give a few of the solutions that were considered and mark one solution as the selected solution. The idea of listing out a few solutions and not just one, is that we acknowledge that when we talk about the "road taken" we must also talk about the "road not taken". This is to focus our discussion with the selected solution on the one hand, and on the other hand to always provide an escape hatch to other ideas once we feel our selected one is not working.

Risks
Risks are a special case of assumptions. These are the assumptions that put this project, product, or customers at risk that we are willing to take. The reason these are assumptions is that risks are not definite – they may or may not happen and the chance of happening is often expressed as a probability.

Out of Scope
List the bodies of work, research, tasks or activities that are out of scope. This is to put the obvious discussions that would be ineffective, out of focus, or counter-productive out of our minds.

Key Metrics
We need to have SMART metrics that test our assumptions, requirements, and ways to solve for our requirements in the right way. Sometimes metrics supports other activities, dependencies, and

sometimes we list out guard metrics that keep us from specifying vanity numbers. For example, we can have a metric to increase website traffic, but we can implement it as just buying the traffic which is bad for churn. To fix it we would also have a metric that guards churn. When specifying metrics we want to: name it, say what it will answer for in a form of a question, as well as how we're going to collect data for it.

Open Questions
List out questions that we know we haven't reached, or subject to continue research given a particular condition, and specify that condition.

— /snip here —

Risk & Complexity

And here's another layer of reality: some tasks and some goals although perfectly planned will *hide* risks. These risks on the best case just hinder execution but on the worst case can fail a project. We see this perhaps the most dramatically in various accidents that happened in the space race and the space program: systems were planned perfectly with zero tolerance and various layers of redundancy, yet they fail. Failure is so important that I have a complete chapter dedicated to learning, and specifically: learning from failure. Here I will focus on what we can do before we get to failing – understanding complexity and risks.

Maybe you built an app that had received so much unexpected success (a good thing!) that you have a database with a billion records and thousands of requests per second that you have never planned to deal with at this stage. You're looking at unaccounted expenses, an expertise you aren't having at the moment, and generally not knowing what to do – and it feels like a ticking time bomb; you reach out for a consultant with a quick response and it probably comes with a price that too, you didn't account for in your budget. On the one side you're overwhelmingly flooded with gratitude for the luck you're having, because, to be successful it's been said you need luck and timing, and you just had one part of it which is 50% of the job. You don't want to lose this in an instant.

So you need to switch to a more scalable database, and you're going to do it on your own. How do you do that? First thing first – in this moments of anxiety and pressure don't trust your gut feelings or knee reactions. You need logic. You need to lay down everything you know about the world, everything you *think* you know, everything that's out there that looks like a solution, list pros and cons, model the solution to your documented requirements, do risk assessment and evaluation, and accommodate, contain, resolve, mitigate, or in other words – find a safe, successful path through a minefield.

Over the years, I've developed an approach for this, helping myself and teams in companies from 30 engineers to hundreds. I called it, unattractively, a "tech spec". It aims to force out human biases, fallacies, and guide you through solid, logical, risk free decision making.

At the end of following the tech spec, filling it out, and answering for every section in it – you should be staring at a path to success. And even if there's a chance you'll fail and you did fail – you're looking at a document showcasing your decision making and you'll be able to back paddle to where you went wrong *and fix only that*, thus quickly iterating and being successful with minimal effort to correct course.

Here's what my tech spec template looks like. You can copy it verbatim and use it as a template for yourself or your organization:

— snip here —

This is a mental tool you should use when doing something which is unknown. This definition includes: POCs, hard problems, new initiatives.

Guidelines to Authors

Remember: everyone can write specs but great specs are short. Not everything here is a must. Motivate yourself and others to collaborate, comment, and document your/their thoughts. Treat this document as a tool, an engineering aid. Not a product or legal document.

Subject

Owner
An owner is responsible to coordinate this document, but not necessarily to provide the solution or content

John Singleton

Collaborators
Who makes the decision (a team? A person?). Who needs to be notified?

Bruce, Lee (decision)
Mark (notify)

Background
Prepare the context and onboard readers. Remember, readers didn't fully immerse themselves in the same way as you did. 3-4 bullets.

Timeline
When is the go-live? When is the first POC? How long can this decision be delayed in order to get more information? Write it down, and set meetings in calendar in correlation to these dates.

Motivation
*Why are we doing this. Is there any chance we don't need to do this at all? (big win A clear statement of the problem (2-3 paragraphs).*J

- Implications:
    - one
    - two

– three

Assumptions

When we identified this as a problem, and when we devised the solution, our reality was very specific. These are the assumptions we took - known and unknown (guesswork) when we approached the problem and devised a solution.

Goals

The primary goal that solves the problem. If there are several primary goals - we have several problems, and we need several independent solutions. Secondary goals are nice-to-haves, or implicitly support other efforts. Each goal should be defined with criteria for success and failure and risks.

- Primary *(just one goal)*
- Secondaries *(a few nice-to-haves but not musts)*

Proposed Solutions

Architecture, engineering, pros/cons, technical and management risks, affected areas and ways to implement. Be specific, but not too specific (i.e. code snippets should live in your repo).

Recommendations

Research results, tips, etc., current issues with POC. What's the next steps.

References

Any link, document, book or even existing old designs that will help others get up to speed

— /snip here —

Principles

Perseverance

When people tell me "you're a genius" I strongly disagree. What I do see myself as is a tortured soul that had meaningful successes here and there. I also tend to go further than what most people find that make sense: I keep going where people would normally stop. So, there's one thing I can say I attribute myself with: perseverance. In other words, I'm not a naturally born genius but I work really hard.

I don't know how to teach perseverance. But I can maybe give you some advice. I can look at myself first: I had a rough childhood in a rough neighborhood, I did competitive bodybuilding, I played a few hard to play and *uncool* instruments (looking at you French Horn) in an orchestra for ten years, and I'm not counting my army service which on itself was one hell of a ride, I served in a confidential army unit where they give me an insane amount of responsibility, and through many rough patches and challenges they got out a leader, just by forces of nature. Today I know that that's what made me have an attribute of perseverance. But if you had the luck of skipping these kind of rough experiences, I'll tell you this: try something hard.

Maybe some kind of extreme sports hobby. Something that'll make you fail that's very physical and visceral and not virtual. I imagine it would be some kind of athletic sports but not only; maybe mountain-bike, rock climbing, indoor climbing, martial arts or something less physical, like painting. Something that will frustrate you so much, that will regularly pose a "brick wall" in front of you that you'll have to overcome – but also that it will happen in a safe place. Nothing bad will happen if you just can't play that scale quickly enough on your guitar, but hey, now you need to answer the question: do you try again? and again? and again?. I think you can build this attribute into you if you want to.

Make Success Effortless

In bodybuilding, it's been said that you have the groups of muscles that you're having a great time with – they react and grow and shape as you want them to with hard but reasonable work, and then there are those groups of muscles that you just can't grow no matter how much effort you put in. It turns out that you have to go above average and above *reasonable* effort to grow these and each individual has their own stories and challenges in that sense. I had a difficult time taming my biceps, arguably the most commonly known groups of muscles (remember Popeye?), we flex these to show we "can do". The thing that changed it for me, is buying a dumbbell, and putting it under my bed. Every morning, the first thing I did was lift that weight. Within eight months I had the biceps I wanted. By having almost no effort to expend to physically get to a gym, I was able to succeed.

I actually stole that trick from Arnold Schwarzenegger. Everyone knows this guy as the man from Terminator ("I'll be back!"), or maybe that odd person with the odd accent. But in fact, when you focus on his bodybuilding career you discover an extremely intelligent athlete that masters both the physical and mental realms.

You just need to know where to find that kind of Arnold. I found his principles and hacks in "The Encyclopedia of Bodybuilding" and in the movie "Pumping Iron". Both niche material that I'm sure not most people know outside of the bodybuilding circles – but trust me, Arnold is a super intelligent, and a natural fan of effectiveness working. No wonder he's been *seven* times Mr. Olympia (the highest title championship in bodybuilding), in the past, where sports weren't that "in our face" as today, some people thought of these competition as a joke, but even if it *was* a joke, back then it took unreasonable, inhumane amounts of work to even get to be qualified to compete.

I take this principle of "Making Success Effortless" to building great APIs. You're probably thinking "wait what? how's bodybuilding related to building great APIs?", well it doesn't, but the principle of the pit of success is. I stole this one from Krzysztof Cwalina, in the seminal work about authoring the .NET framework, titled "Framework Design Guidelines".

This principle goes like this: you want developers not to climb a mountain to be successful (how we're all get taught about how success look like), but to "fall into a pit of success" which is *effortless.*

If I build an object using a builder method, I want to magically "just know" what's the next method I should call. Can I name the object in a way that helps? Can I use a different technique? (e.g. fluent interface) Do I even need a new object for someone to remember? And finally, I always like to ask "how many concepts I'm forcing people to remember" and "how do they start" and "how do they get something done in just 1-2-3?". Force your API into these principles and you just applied the "principle of least effort", or the "pit of success", or "making success effortless" – they all mean the same.

Set time to actively seek the pit of success in everything you do for others as well as for yourself. In many ways automation is one shape of applying that. Finding that you're using the same website to get updated in tech news every day and that it often leads you to procrastinate and move on to other websites? get an IFTTT ("if this then that") account, pull the website RSS into a daily email digest. This way you have an hour where the news is being pushed to you, and you're in your email. You read the news, and get it done with.

Of course a word has to be said about Email being counter-productive, but what i'm saying assumes you treat your email as a strict place where you go in and go out rather quickly. If you don't, that's another practice to cover later.

Immersion

It's fairly well known that the easiest way to learn a new language is by traveling to and living in a country that speaks the language you want to learn. This is the principle of full immersion. If you've managed to design your goals, life achievements that entertain these goals, and broken up your goals to tasks, then you have to provide some kind of immersive fuel. If you're building the next RPG game, make sure you are flooded with RPG news, read RPG news, talk about RPG in family dinners, and so on. This will give you the implicit motivation for your goals. There comes a moment when you're deep into a goal that you'll start doubting what you're doing – we're trying to never arrive at that moment by surrounding ourselves with a sense of purpose *all the time*, and building "insurance policies" so that our friends know that *this is what we do* now, and when we move off the path, they'll make sure to nudge us back in like great friends do.

Beware that there's also a downside to this. By building lean, or sticking to a startup mantra of embracing change, full immersion is something that can hinder change. You already told everyone you're doing the RPG (Role Playing Game) app, your professional network thinks of you as the RPG expert. What happens if RPG as a domain just crashes, and your idea becomes useless as a result?

In fact, you have to take that into account with every goal you set. So you won't have a successful RPG app, but you'll still have valuable experience in: making an app, "living" in a market you are new to, the connections you've made in RPG that might be usable in your next thing, and technical knowledge such as graphics, 3D and more.

Often, people who undergo this kind of pivot, move on to a completely unrelated but somewhat technically related field – and become very successful there. I built an experimentation platform three times in the Adtech industry, where it was a standard thing, however not until I built an experimentation platform for a big Fintech unicorn that my platform was perceived as ground-breaking. I was bringing a trusted, production-ready technology and principles to a different domain that was very hungry for it, and in fact, made a radically new use of it. Personally, when I realized that this is what I did, it was quite exciting.

Learn

On the spectrum of your various activities that surround work, there's one kind of activity that takes a significant amount of time, cannot be rushed, and has (almost) no shortcuts: learning. If it takes a large amount of time, it would be the most effective way to optimize it, right?

Learn Effectively

Let's review a few principles for *learning effectively*. First thing's first:

You can't rush learning.

Sorry, speed readers, gist writers, tldr;'ers, and various other instant-glory and snake-oil solutions to a centuries old problem – that by the way, became *a problem* only now, in the information age, and only in the last 10-20 years when we've managed to build ourselves an information industry that is well-connected, real-time, and that is never off line and never stops working.

On the other hand, learning the hard way *is* effective. Find ways to learn the hard way: your brain is much more primed to receive and embed new information when it's frustrating. Don't follow a tutorial. Try to build something, fail, and fail, and then go do that tutorial. Find a project and focus on building that project, fail, and fail, and *then* remember that your real goal is to learn something new. Learning will happen as a side-effect.

Well, if you *still* want shortcuts, try bundling learning with something else. For example, if you want to learn to program, and you're also learning to play the guitar, try to make a chord generator, or maybe something a bit more challenging (but fun!) like a chord analyzer where it tells you what you're playing. This way you're combining the two learning curves together and investing time in both efforts rather one at a time.

This means the shortcuts you're taking are not in learning itself, but in using the time for learning in an effective way. This is the general theme of this book.

There are no silver bullets, but there are plenty of inefficiencies in how we work.

Here's another shortcut: find experienced people and learn all their secrets. Plain and simple. Here, learning is easy, but finding experienced people that are doing things *properly* is extremely hard.

Maintain a learning path and a learning log, which means to set aside time to proactively create learning paths and opportunities to learn.

You'll need to set time to find interesting *and effective* courses and put them on a "to-do list", generate a stream of articles in your topics of interest to go deep on. Every now and then make an incursion into a topic that you are not familiar with professionally but are mildly interested with (e.g. baking), so that you can find that gap-bridge of opportunity (e.g. build a baking timer, or neural network for saying when bread is baked well) of making interesting learning projects, whilst helping someone or, more frankly speaking – making money.

Set Learning Expectations

Say you're about to hit a trove of knowledge: say you want to learn data science. Sometimes the go-to action is to, well, pick a book and get reading and read effectively and quickly right?. Wrong.

Treat this like any other working task, and set expectations between yourself and, well, yourself.

Write down in bullets your action plan towards this new knowledge base, such as what you expect to learn, or in other words:

- Augmenting your existing knowledge: reinforcing what you know, filling up for things you didn't know. Write down these in notes as you go through the material.
- Steal things (In the Picasso sense, *"Good artists copy; great artists steal"*). There might be ideas that you can take wholesale. Write these down as they happen.
- Business ideas. Don't forget that even if you're trying to learn something new, you are still, in the larger sense, in this for the business. Keep your eyes peeled for easy, new, or different business ideas the material you're going through might provoke.
- Getting nothing. Be prepared for wasting your time. Some knowledge bases are useless for reasons such as low-quality up to low-relevance. Try to mark down what isn't useful, and to avoid it for the next time or as you go.
- Remember: when spending time learning, time will fly and so time is your enemy. Treat it with suspicion: set a timer / use Pomodoro[12] to remind you you're in a rabbit hole. It'll align your brain to be effective and not be pulled into a "passing time reading for fun" mode.
- Use pen and paper. The tactile feel and physical properties of pen and paper disconnects your brain from "reading time" and connects it to "I'm working towards a goal" mode. Even if you throw the paper out later, the experience will still stick.

---

[12]https://en.wikipedia.org/wiki/Pomodoro_Technique

How to Read Books

In order to learn, you can read blogs, watch videos on YouTube, have an online course as part of a MOOC, or just a quick ten minute course on something very specific. However books are in my eyes, a special category. This medium of knowledge capture and transfer exist the longest, and has the most miles, and in turn, attracts the most serious talents to disclose the most serious bodies of knowledge. However, it turns out that not all books are of good quality, and this is becoming more true as the competing media such as blogs and instant videos take stage.

It's up to you to find the better books.

There was a time where humanity only had books. In 1940 the classic "How To Read a Book"[13] was published, and it dealt with the question of how to consume what was the *only* kind of media that held serious bodies of knowledge at the time: books.

It makes sense, people surrounded with books wanting to read books more effectively and that book *reading* was a serious skill to have, just as searching Google effectively today is a serious skill to have. Notice the difference in approaches? Today, we're hunting data, not consuming it, and I'm afraid that the more we hunt for data the more we forget how to effectively consume it.

I'm going to present my own version of *How To Read a Book* that is more updated with the books we have today and how we operate today (for example, with electronic books we no longer need an index).

In the original work, there were four reading stages:

1. Elementary - looking at the cover, table of contents, pick a random point, read a bit, and then straight to Chapter One. This is what most of us do.

---

[13]https://en.wikipedia.org/wiki/How_to_Read_a_Book

2. Inspectional - in this mode, we acknowledge that reading a book is a multi-pass process, which is very different from what most of us do. We will give it a skim, read a bit from each chapter to get a clue of what we're dealing with, the writing style, and the general sense of quality

3. Analytical - in this mode, we're treating our reading as research. We state a few questions before reading more deeply. Such as what question is the writer posing and how will they answer it throughout.

4. Syntopic - the most advanced according to the original authors. In this mode you'll be picking up every important book on the subject and perform a comparison side-by side of the arguments made, getting only the best from all books.

First off I believe that, arguably, *Syntopic* reading is no longer necessary these days. We have crowd sourced this to a great degree and it's enough to understand how reviews of a book fare and how people would break down the correct volume for us.

So this is what I focus on:

1. Inspectional - focus on table of contents, the perform a skim read of the book or parts of it, just as the original text prescribed.

2. Analytical - in this part I'm getting ready for deep reads. I would still not read cover-to-cover unless I find the writing style from part (1) lucid and enjoyable, in which case I would dive head first for a cover-to-cover read. Otherwise, for each chapter I would write down questions for myself that I *think* I'll get answers for, just by reading the title and the first abstract part of the chapter. It doesn't matter if I hit on target, what matters is that because I know I have questions to answer, I keep myself sharp and focused and have a purposeful read. It's also a small form of gamification - did I guess what this chapter is talking about?

Biases

To be able to learn well, as well as execute well, it's best to know where we often are misled by our natural biases. Let's look at the most popular ones.

The Sunk Cost Effect / Loss Aversion

This family of biases describes the way we tend to undervalue or overvalue something, and to rationalize over it because of what looks like our basic psychological properties, such as the fear of appearing as "losers", or peer pressure, or pressure and expectations from ourselves and so on. For example, we tend to continue doing something even though factually it doesn't really return on our investment anymore.

Simple examples:

- Keep reading a book although it sucks.
- Keep betting at a casino although you're losing.

The challenge here is that we tend to *rationalize* our bias to ourselves and we keep doing what eventually isn't helpful to ourselves.

This bias is *extremely* important for working effectively. Since time is one of your most valuable assets, this bias, if you're not aware of it, will cause serious time waste.

I see this every day. Since I bootstrap many of my projects, I run a strong risk of continuing a project even though it has no business value anymore, which happens deep into running a project because I've got onto a stage of discovery that I couldn't have gotten onto if I hadn't invested *serious* efforts in already. With that in mind, comes that I *have* to know how to kill a project.

Take this book for example. Since I'm quite immune to this bias, I've started this book as a draft. Then as a blog post which I shared internally. Then as cafeteria talks and phone calls. Then as a single or couple chapters which I shared. And so on. I *incrementally* and hesitantly built my confidence and made sure that, at every step of the way, I'm not falling into a sunk cost effect.

So every step of the journey of writing this book, which took around half a year to a year, was validated and made in a safe way – where *I reserve the right* to drop everything in the trash at any given moment in order to not fall into the sunk cost effect and by that to invest further into something that will never grow as I want it to.

Optimism Bias

Until I found out, read, and researched this bias, people saw me as the ultra realist. Perhaps sometimes mixed realism with pessimism. But now I can say, I'm not negative or pessimistic. I just full recognized and strive to be immune to the optimism bias.

From Wikipedia:

"Optimism bias is a cognitive bias that causes someone to believe that they themselves are less likely to experience a negative event. It is also known as unrealistic optimism or comparative optimism."

And this is why it happens, again from Wikipedia:

"Four factors exist that cause a person to be optimistically biased: their desired end state, their cognitive mechanisms, the information they have about themselves versus others, and overall mood"

Mood. Really? so what will determine success in a project or working effectively will be *your mood* at the moment of making a decision. As a realist and logical person I want to believe that this is wrong. There has to be a more scientific way to make decisions.

The first step, is to recognize and acknowledge the *optimism bias*. The way to resolve this bias is to come up with a structured way to think and make decisions, a framework if you will. We talk about this later in this book, and about how *technical specs* help you to make the right decisions bias-free in the tech world.

The Ambiguity Effect

We tend to stay away from things we don't know. But the more sophisticated version of this that hurt us in software and in tech: we will not consider technology that can *really* help us, just because we haven't taken the time to study it. And so, through my consulting work, I've managed to pick a ton of low-hanging fruit by breaking down a company's tech posture, understanding where they compromised because of fear of the unknown, swapping that out, and coming back with a 10x more productive engineering organization.

From Wikipedia:

"The ambiguity effect is a cognitive bias where decision making is affected by a lack of information, or "ambiguity". The effect implies that people tend to select options for which the probability of a favorable outcome is known, over an option for which the probability of a favorable outcome is unknown."

The way to counter this effect is to invest time in researching what we don't know, and clear the forest out of risks.

The way we suggest to do this in this book is by having special purpose tasks called E&E's, or Explore & Experiment which is a strong intention that's timed and "budgeted" for exploring the unknown (you'll read more about this further out in the book).

Anchoring

Welcome to what magic tricks count on. They "anchor" you to a reality, get you fixated, while the real trick is being done "behind the scenes".

In more realistic terms, in our industry, anchoring is when we stick to what we *know*; which is kind of the opposite of the *ambiguity effect* (see why I like this domain? you can start to identify patterns and distributions between biases).

To counter anchoring, like many of the human biases by the way, you can use a few more people and probe into their opinions. So by power of *averaging* you get closer to reality.

If you think a task is very hard and will take a week to perform, and another person thinks it takes a day, well probably each person comes from a different background and perspective and is anchored to a different opinion. If we take an average we can play it "safe" in determining what's really the effort needed to perform that given task.

Of course, it's not that simple, but then you need to factor in the *domain*, the task, the context for performing the task, and many other variables that affect proper estimation of effort (there will be more about estimations later in the book).

NIH (Not Invented Here) Syndrome

You might have heard that engineers like to reinvent the wheel. That's a common frustration among technical and non-technical people: why not use something that's free and that's out there and has good quality? why build your own?

Many times the reasoning to building your own will be very detailed and would kind of make sense; while reasoning to buying or using something that already exists wouldn't be that detailed.

Engineers would naturally want to investigate and "dive in" into building rather than "dive in" into buying, after all they're attracted to solving hard problems (as I can testify for myself).

But behind this, there's a general bias that hits all of us, not only engineers, and that's the "IKEA Effect": people will tend to place *more value* into something that they participated in creating.

Some times, smart Product people will use this to create a "sticky" product. We did this in one of the products we were building. We built a launcher, lock-screen, and other OS-level enhancements for Android that are custom-made and give you an added value of a world of content that's personalized to your interests. Kind of Android-meets-Google-news.

We had a dilemma: lockscreens are *very* intrusive. You install them and the experience of *opening your phone* changes fundamentally. Our first mistake? we branded our default lock screen to *our* heart's content: we wanted to show all our UX skills and abilities. It turns out that if you had a picture of your kids on your lock screen we replaced it with our logo. Wow, what a mistake.

So we changed course: let our user tweak and configure everything. We changed the product to be super configurable and we didn't come with an opinion about how the default design should be. You (1) install the product (2) immediately configure it. Now, it turns out, people that went through the effort of configuration – perceived our lockscreen as *theirs*, not *ours*. Lesson learned!

So there are two takeaways here:

1. Sometimes engineers *do* reinvent the wheel. When we list the pros/cons of "build vs buy" we need someone to balance the passion for building our own in the loop.
2. Still, sometimes it's worth to go for "build" to generate a fundamental sense of ownership. But that's a sociological and not a technological aspect.

The Planning Fallacy

In 1979, my two idols: Tversky and Kahneman published a series of research papers, in which they identified the planning fallacy, from Wikipedia: *"a phenomenon in which predictions about how much time will be needed to complete a future task display an optimism bias and underestimate the time needed"*.

Or in other words, as we all have seen this in buildings, roads, and the likes: we tend to underestimate the time needed to complete a task.

How to counter this? break down to smaller tasks. It's been shown that when you take a task and estimate, and then break it down into an array of smaller tasks and estimate those and sum up their estimations, you get the following result:

The time estimate of the large unbroken task will be smaller than the *sum* of the broken up, smaller tasks that in total compose the needed work for the large task.

The Semmelweis Reflex

This bias shows that we're averse to accepting new evidence about something that's already a norm or is already the status-quo. In other words, we lack the energy to challenge our day-to-day.

The lesson learned here is what Apple already showed us in the now widely known 80's and 90's slogan: *Think Different*.

Or in a more practical sense, there's value for working effectively here. You need to challenge how you work every now and then to gain incremental improvement. For me? I feel safe to throw away hard-earned work just to adopt a newer, radical, better ways of working if they deliver on their promise.

Bikeshedding

Also known as "Law of Triviality". It states that when faced with something hard, people will naturally focus on the easy things that don't really make a difference, and value these as more important.

We've all seen it: need to migrate a ton of legacy code? – sure but would we use tabs or spaces? with or without semicolons? what's the new code style?

Enter weeks of meetings and discussion about the new code style that we want to move to. And before you know it, we used up all of the time needed to actually *perform* the legacy code migration. What happens next? you guessed it – everyone rushes to migrate the old code, and because there's not enough time to do anything properly, they pick a bad code style and practices quickly, rush to implement, and effectively – create a *new legacy codebase* with marginal improvement over the old or none at all. Such is the comedy of software engineering – because you're not seeing the material you're wasting (such as with woodworking for example), you have very little awareness to waste.

To counter this effectively, you need to be aware of this fallacy. Identify it, make others aware of it, and stop the discussion – make a decision, any decision about code style and move on.

In fact, just focusing a little bit more about code styles, there's a movement of "standard code style" and "one formatter to rule them all" in languages, that makes you adopt just a single code style, with no ability to customize it – take it or leave it. For example Go, the programming language made by Google, gives you just a single tool to format your code and the style rules are very strict with no ability to customize. No more will there be discussions about code style – Google thought. And they were right. I can't imagine how much time this has saved organizations. Well played, Google!

Zero Risk Bias

This bias is the tendency to place more value for going from *little risk* to *zero risk*, rather than *big risk* to *little risk*. People will go above and beyond to invest in eliminating risk completely and will not accept the fact that *there's always risk*.

The way to counter that is to work with numbers and statistics. How does a certain risk look in numbers? what are the implications?

For example, there's a 30% risk of a cyber breach that will result in over 10M records exposed which means $10M in damages.

We ought to present a few more questions. For example, is there a cyber insurance? if so, the risk to the company is less than what we thought. By that, did we bring the 30% number to 5% risk of insurance not covering the loss? great job done – let's handle the next 30% huge risk target that we find.

It's better to work in this kind of workflow, instead of taking the 5% risk and driving it to the bottom, missing the fact that we actually have a bunch of 30% risks scattered around the organizations in other places.

Availability Bias

People tend to place more value on what they remember last. It seems that we think that facts that we remember are important, otherwise why would we remember them?

In actuality, the topic of *importance* has nothing to do with our ability to remember or memorize. We might remember a logging product because it has a cute beaver as its logo, our mind will trick us into thinking it's a good product because, well, otherwise why would it leave such a strong impression?

To counter the availability bias, we have to develop a system to evaluate whether something is important (or good, or has more

value, or more critical, etc.) or not. whether it's considering pros/-
cons, or keeping notes, or performing POCs – even though we're
completely sure of what the result would be – are essential to proper
and effective work.

Can you think of great product logos that feature cute animals in
them that made an impression on you? Is the product itself *good*?
Did you think it was good up until now that you've discovered the
availability bias?

Wrong decisions make for a waste of time. A waste of time makes
for ineffective work. Our *wrong* decisions are influenced in part by
our hard-coded human fallacies and biases.

Learn How to Fail

There are three aspects to failing *effectively*:

1. Fail fast
2. Recovery
3. Learning from failure

Since these are part culture part technology and part design and
architecture, each of these is a monumental effort to practice in an
already running engineering organization.

However it is relatively easy when you're building a new company,
organization or creating a new team. And even more so if you just
want to apply these for yourself to work more effectively.

Failing Fast

So what's failing fast? let's look at failing slowly. Here's a fictional
algorithm and story:

```
1    1. Download FOREX sheet
2    2. Download monetary conversion tables
3    3. Prepare training data
4    4. Normalize FOREX data with conversion tables
5    5. Enrich training data with FOREX data
6    6. Train
7    7. Run a test set to calculate accuracy KPIs
```

So let's say (2) can fail. A resourceful engineer would do this:

```
1    1. Download FOREX sheet
2    2. Download monetary conversion tables
3    2.1 if failed, try again
4    2.2 if failed, go to backups and load a stored file from \
5    previous run
6    2.3 if no backup, send an email to admin and wait in a lo\
7    op
8    2.4 check again if there's a backup, if existing resume
9    2.5 before resuming, check again if the internet works
10
11   ... and so on ...
```

The *fail fast* approach would go like this:

```
1    1. Download FOREX sheet
2    2. Download monetary conversion tables
3    2.1 if failed, try again
4    2.2 if failed, output trace data, crash and terminate
```

A *master* process would identify a crash and restart the whole process as is, without trying to "figure out" what's wrong and build exceptional flows into the system.

Failing fast gives you:

1. Simple code

2. Great traceability data to figure out what went wrong

3. A simple recovery model

As you might sense, *simplicity* is a very important factor when failing or in a failed state. As this is an exceptional state, you don't want too many factors, such as understanding convoluted error recovery code involved to make a complex and exceptional situation even more complex.

That approach, for example, is what Erlang took for its modus operandi. Erlang is a programming language that powers zero-downtime, critical systems, telecom mainframes and more around the world since the 80's and 90's. It's still running strong today, for example – it powers a great deal of WhatsApp, and is one of the greatest success factors for Klarna, a Fintech unicorn I've worked for.

Failing fast in Erlang is one of the pillars of its production operation. I can say from first-hand experience, it really makes a difference for robust, production grade distributed systems.

You'll have to *chase* failing fast. In every flow, every artifact: a web service, a logging framework, a mobile app, and even a client-side frontend application. The opportunity for complex error recovery code versus the "crash and halt" fail fast approach is always there. Once you're aware of failing fast you can be the guardian of it and make sure at least the discussion is always there. On the worst case you'll save a lot of code from being written, in the best case you'll make a robust software system.

Recovery

Recovery is the ability to go from a failed state to a healthy one in a safe way. It doesn't mean it needs to happen *fast*, just *safe*. What's unsafe? well, there's a *flapping failure* condition where a system crashes, gets up, hits a problem, crashes, gets up, hits a problem, crashes and so on. As you might imagine monitoring solutions either identify *flapping* processes or not. In the case where these monitoring solutions aren't aware of this condition – you're out of luck. Basically, these systems will "fall" on the healthy state randomly and on the failing state randomly (as the process keeps failing and getting back up), and that will create a great deal of production noise, false positives, false negatives, and well, you get the point.

So we want to recover *safely*. In order to do that you need to output the only bit of information that's important to you: the reality you see *before* failing, and after. We call that the failure context.

To recap, recovery means you:

1. Move from failed to healthy state safely
2. Output the information you need to do (1) *and* to be able to reason about moving from failed to healthy

It might sound simple but it *can* be complex. You'll need to trace process, apply a tiered layer of monitoring, have your existing infrastructure support monitoring and tracing, ship all that data reliably, and so on. In the context of an organization, you'll need an *engineering effectiveness* group to think hard about this, and apply it. Being an individual, you can pick up Google's SRE that (well, Google that, no pun intended), which is a fantastic book and something great you can do to your career and approach about working effectively.

Learning From Failure

I view learning from failure as a competitive advantage for an engineering organization, and then in turn for the organization itself. An organization that knows how to investigate, fix, and learn effectively is one that can beat any competition more quickly than the opposite. In a race to win, every company makes its share of mistakes, and you'll just finish up your share more quickly.

Google's SRE book is a great guidance for this (mentioned in the previous section), and I give out courses and training which I call the "Learning Failing Engineering Organization" (FLEO for short). Personally I'm fascinated about failing, I research NASA's *lessons learned* library for my own fun (google that), I research battles and combat and history (I believe intense situations are a great place to extract decision making insights from). I am also a fan of Sidney Dekker, a person who researches failures and investigation of failures (airline failures specifically), which you can also Google and pick up his seminal book: *"The Field Guide to Human Error"*.

I also believe each engineering organization should have a domain dedicated to failing just like it has for proper architecture, delivering on time, and delivering business value; whether it's training, culture or tooling. I gives these the appropriate focus in my FLEO course.

Appendix

Quick Hacks For When You Can't Start

- Remember you have two fears, and the fear of making a mistake is overcoming the fear of starting - set a virtual deadline, or any kind of stimulant: the fear of losing money, face, or reputation works
- When you can't start, start 10 minutes of a task
- When you can't start, find big tasks and break these down into smaller tasks
- If you have some time to kill, go over tasks and make sure they're: properly labeled and filled out, and you have a definition of done, as well as an actionable title (the first step in the task spelled out as the title)
- Pick a task that deals with building support for starting tasks more easily, such as building a starter-project for promo websites.
- Plan actively for tomorrow
- Use Pomodoro or another way to make sure you're aware that you're diving into a rabbit hole – and if so, be able to step away and not fall into a time sink

Daily Sprint Execution

- Random idea? random raw task?
  * Less than 2m? do it
  * Can't do it? let someone else do it, delegate

* Can do it? great!

* Translate into a visible and physical action (maybe the first action that starts the task) + include needed resources in body (articles, videos, emails, names, phone numbers)
* Put under JIRA backlog, under the relevant epic, if it's a clear epic-based task finish here.
* If it's a vague, non-epic, non-goal, thinking/planning, soft task put it in Evernote Incoming. If you're promoting Incoming to Next, you want to classify, just like in GTD:
* Workflow: indicate what kind of "next" this is: writing, reading, etc.
* Objective/Project: give it one label based on the project or objective it belongs to, and should "account under"
* Context: give it a context tag such as "#code", if a person use @person-name (and/or @company-name or @place) this helps pull all notes when speaking to someone or in social interactions
* ONLY IF CRITICAL move to 'now'

- If it's morning, perform an E&E task (explore and experiment)
  * It's reasonable that after you explore an idea you end up with a bunch of new ideas or tasks. These go to your Evernote inbox or JIRA backlog respectively
- Otherwise pick a task from the current JIRA sprint and execute
- Stick to these sprint job-stealing/shuffling rules as you browse through the daily work, and around the sprint:
    - If you can't execute, groom – break tasks, tag them, estimate them, prioritize them, or start just 10 minutes out of a certain task.
    - If you're about to finish a sprint, locate a dead-easy task, a "hot" task, and instead of going for the easy target, push it to the next sprint so you have a great 'landing

zone' for bridging your productivity from current sprint to the next sprint

- If you finished a sprint, you should be looking at the retro task now which every sprint should contain: just a task called "retro"; that's all that remains, stop here and rest. Do the retro the next day and make sure you're energetic.

- During mid-day perform your GTD crunch, and sprint crunch
  - In Evernote, sort out your inbox and "now": kill irrelevant tasks, or promote tasks to JIRA backlog
  - In JIRA, go over your backlog: kill irrelevant tasks, break tasks into smaller ones, promote tasks into the next sprint or demote tasks out of the current sprint
- Scan your calendar for meetings. Meetings are important since they break up your productivity and influences your sprint execution.
- Scan your Waiting-for and Tickler notebooks in Evernote (for Waiting-for and Tickler see here[14])

Sprint Closing Checklist

List out:

- 3 things that went well
- 3 things that went badly
- what goals were advanced the most
- what held you back from executing the most
- what goals were not advanced as they should
- 3 ideas to improve workflow

Act:

---

[14]https://hamberg.no/gtd/

- Pick 1 item to improve + schedule to current sprint
- Pick 1 item to serve as workflow optimization + schedule current sprint
- Pick 1 item to help unblocking
- Prioritize one task from a goal that was starved
- Declare the goal for the next sprint in one sentence and name the sprint according to that

Weekly Trigger Checklist

Here are a bunch of keywords to get you started:

- Projects
- Boss
- Co-workers
- Projects started, not completed
- Projects that need to be started
- People I need to get back to
- Social events: meetups
- Saying thanks to people
- Go over "burning" Github issues
- Look for new conferences, podcasts sources for gym and running
- Tech news
- Go over book recommendations
- Focus note — what do i want to do in life

Product Feature Spec Template

Spec Title

Goal
The goal state should "set the atmosphere", set the business value in

clear terms, and supply reason for: (1) why do it (2) why now.

Use Cases / Requirements

Supply a structured list of use cases in the typical BDD format: "As a /persona/ I want to be able to /perform goal/ in order to /business value/". In many cases this can be a table, linking a user story to a JIRA epic (use any other issue tracker you like).

Assumptions

Supply a list of hypothesis or assumptions. We want to be able to list everything we know about the world that can explain why we wrote this spec the way we wrote it. The goal here is, given a mistake, to be able to correct it quickly.

Solutions Considered

Give a few of the solutions that were considered and mark one solution as the selected solution. The idea of listing out a few solutions and not just one, is that we acknowledge that when we talk about the "road taken" we must also talk about the "road not taken". This is to focus our discussion with the selected solution on the one hand, and on the other hand to always provide an escape hatch to other ideas once we feel our selected one is not working.

Risks

Risks are a special case of assumptions. These are the assumptions that put this project, product, or customers at risk that we are willing to take. The reason these are assumptions is that risks are not definite – they may or may not happen and the chance of happening is often expressed as a probability.

Out of Scope

List the bodies of work, research, tasks or activities that are out of scope. This is to put the obvious discussions that would be ineffective, out of focus, or counter-productive out of our minds.

Key Metrics

We need to have SMART metrics that test our assumptions, requirements, and ways to solve for our requirements in the right way. Sometimes metrics supports other activities, dependencies, and sometimes we list out guard metrics that keep us from specifying vanity numbers. For example, we can have a metric to increase website traffic, but we can implement it as just buying the traffic which is bad for churn. To fix it we would also have a metric that guards churn. When specifying metrics we want to: name it, say what it will answer for in a form of a question, as well as how we're going to collect data for it.

Open Questions

List out questions that we know we haven't reached, or subject to continue research given a particular condition, and specify that condition.

Tech Spec Template

This is a mental tool you should use when doing something which is unknown. This definition includes: POCs, hard problems, new initiatives.

Guidelines to Authors

Remember: everyone can write specs but great specs are short. Not everything here is a must. Motivate yourself and others to collaborate, comment, and document your/their thoughts. Treat this document as a tool, an engineering aid. Not a product or legal document.

Subject

Owner

An owner is responsible to coordinate this document, but not necessarily to provide the solution or content

John Singleton

Collaborators

Who makes the decision (a team? A person?). Who needs to be notified?

Bruce, Lee (decision)
Mark (notify)

Background
Prepare the context and onboard readers. Remember, readers didn't fully immerse themselves in the same way as you did. 3-4 bullets.

Timeline
When is the go-live? When is the first POC? How long can this decision be delayed in order to get more information? Write it down, and set meetings in calendar in correlation to these dates.

Motivation
Why are we doing this. Is there any chance we don't need to do this at all? (big win A clear statement of the problem (2-3 paragraphs).

- Implications:
  - one
  - two
  - three

Assumptions
When we identified this as a problem, and when we devised the solution, our reality was very specific. These are the assumptions we took - known and unknown (guesswork) when we approached the problem and devised a solution.

Goals
The primary goal that solves the problem. If there are several primary goals - we have several problems, and we need several independent solutions. Secondary goals are nice-to-haves, or implicitly support other efforts. Each goal should be defined with criteria for success and failure and risks.

- Primary *(just one goal)*

- Secondaries *(a few nice-to-haves but not musts)*

Proposed Solutions
Architecture, engineering, pros/cons, technical and management risks, affected areas and ways to implement. Be specific, but not too specific (i.e. code snippets should live in your repo).

Recommendations
Research results, tips, etc., current issues with POC. What's the next steps.

References
Any link, document, book or even existing old designs that will help others get up to speed

Made in the USA
Middletown, DE
19 January 2022

59102612R00080